CHESHIRE INN SIGNS

The Bells of Peover, Lower Peover, was the local of the American Third Army, which was stationed in the area during the Second World War, before moving to the south coast to take part in the D-Day landings. Generals Eisenhower and Patten, who made Over Peover Hall their headquarters, also made use of the pub. General Patten gave permission for the Stars and Stripes to be flown at the pub, so that to this day the British and American flags fly together.

CHESHIRE INN SIGNS

JOAN P. ALCOCK

For Susan and Julian Baines, long-standing friends, who helped to seek out and record some difficult to find inn signs for this book.

Cover illustrations. Front, from left to right, top: *Abbey Arms, Delamere; Crown Inn, Lower Peover; The Swan, Wybunbury.* Bottom: *The Wilsons, Runcorn; The Vine, Shavington; Ye Olde White Lion, Congleton.* Back: *The Plough, Eaton near Congleton.*

First published 2008

The History Press
The Mill, Brimscombe Port
Stroud, Gloucestershire, GL5 2QG
www.thehistorypress.co.uk

© Joan P. Alcock, 2008

The right of Joan P. Alcock to be identified as the Author of this work has been asserted in accordance with the Copyrights, Designs and Patents Act 1988.

All rights reserved. No part of this book may be reprinted or reproduced or utilised in any form or by any electronic, mechanical or other means, now known or hereafter invented, including photocopying and recording, or in any information storage or retrieval system, without the permission in writing from the Publishers.
British Library Cataloguing in Publication Data.
A catalogue record for this book is available from the British Library.

ISBN 978 0 7524 4770 4

Typesetting and origination by The History Press
Printed in Great Britain

CONTENTS

Foreword & Acknowledgements　　7

Introduction　　11

A-Z of Cheshire Inn Signs　　15

FOREWORD & ACKNOWLEDGEMENTS

When *London Inn Signs* was published in 2007, I said that it had been a difficult book to write not because of the pleasure of seeking out inn signs but because it has been a frustrating and somewhat sad journey to note how many signs are disappearing, pubs closing, some being demolished, some to be converted into houses, shops and offices, and others being taken over by chains which have no interest in keeping historic signs. This is also happening in Cheshire and it is a great pity, perhaps a tragedy, because many names reflect facets of the county – local families, events and its history.

When a brewery chain replaces a sign, even if this is of a cartoon character or a complete travesty of the old sign, it can still be acceptable. It is when the sign disappears completely or is replaced by a sign bearing only the name that there is a feeling of loss. When a pub closes, a piece of the history of the village, town or the county has vanished. So much is changing that it cannot be guaranteed that seekers after inn signs will find the same sign, a sign or even the pub in place from one visit to the next. Many pubs have changed their name several times over the years and where possible this has been recorded in this book, as has any change in sign.

Many pubs in Cheshire began as farmhouses where, in order to make a living, a farmer would begin to brew beer. Local landowners who wanted to provide a living for their tenants founded other pubs. Landlords were then only too grateful to use their patron's coat of arms as a sign. Pubs served as courthouses, were used to try petty offences, housed inquests, acted as vestries for churches and as billets for soldiers. The English Civil War, which took place from 1642 to 1649, divided the people of Cheshire, especially prominent local families, who had to choose between loyalty to the King and to Parliament. Battles and skirmishes took place with several pubs being used by one side or the other or being witness to local feuds.

Inns provided casual refreshment for locals, acted as a meeting place for Friendly Societies, hosts to the local hunts and often (especially in east Cheshire) provided shelter from inclement weather. Many pubs in Cheshire were founded or adapted as coaching inns from the 1660s to 1840 when coaches were the fastest way of travelling in the country. The 1663 Turnpike Act had ensured that some improvements were made to what had been muddy track ways. Later road builders, such as Blind Jack of Knaresborough and John Macadam, improved the condition of the roads, so that an expected service of coaches could take passengers throughout Britain. The 1755 Turnpike Act inaugurated a huge programme of repairs, and improvements to every type of vehicle ensured faster speeds were achieved, meaning that a coach could make fifty to eighty miles a day. Enterprising entrepreneurs soon established regular coach runs.

Inns provided regular stopping places where passengers could board or leave their coach and where refreshment and lodging were provided. The inn became the social hub of a town or village where the latest news was disseminated. Cheshire was an important staging post on the London and Birmingham coach runs to Liverpool, Manchester and the North, which explains the large number of coaching inns in Cheshire. Inn yards bustled with life, as an army of servants appeared to wait on hungry travellers desperate for food, warmth and comfort.

This was not destined to last for long. In the early nineteenth century the digging of canals and the construction of the railways brought a different kind of transport, which resulted in the termination of the stage-coaching era. The result was a proliferation of canal-side and railway station public houses. Canals, especially the Trent and Mersey Canal, the Bridgwater Canal and the Shropshire Union Canal, were very important for the carriage of goods. After 1840, however, the far faster railway traffic ensured the demise of the slower canal commercial trade, but pleasure boating in this century has given a second chance for survival of the canal-side pubs. Railway station pubs often had stables so that travellers could continue their journeys on horseback or by hiring a coach or a chaise.

The industrial growth of towns resulted in small pubs being built for the working class; these still survive, often situated at street corners where they performed a useful adjunct to street architecture. Many retain their original features; others have been renovated or have been rebuilt. Motoring has also provided country pubs with a new clientele, so that public houses can continue to offer accommodation and hospitality for individuals, to social groups and for functions. This is particularly the case in rural Cheshire where a country pub can often survive on its reputation for good food beyond the local area. The locals do not always welcome a makeover to a gastro pub although it may bring in a different kind of customer from further afield.

Given the size of Cheshire it is impossible to cover every sign. There would also be a great deal of repetition. The area covered is that of the present county of Cheshire as defined by the local government reform in 1974, together with its unitary authorities. In the reform Cheshire lost part of Wirral and some of its northern area. The author has taken the liberty, however, of including a few remarkable public houses and inn

The Cheshire Cheese, Wheelock. *Cheshire Cat, Christleton.*

signs, which were once in the historic county of Cheshire. In 2009 the county of Cheshire will be divided into East Cheshire and West Cheshire with some uncertainty as to what this will entail in the matter of the historic county government. Given these considerations, it is important that a representative selection has been made of the more interesting or historic Cheshire signs. The choice is therefore selective but it is hoped that it will encourage the reader to seek out and note inn signs together with the history of their origin.

I am most grateful to all the innkeepers, publicans and drinkers who answered what seemed to be curious questions; to Brenda Rose and Sue and Julian Baines who sought out inn signs, to Helga Pihlakas who proofread the manuscript, to Maureen Walsh who helped to sort out the photographs and to Barbara Kern who assisted with checking text and photographs. All the photographs have been taken by the author and remain her copyright.

INTRODUCTION

'There is no private house, in which people can enjoy themselves, so much as in a capital tavern… No Sir, there is nothing which has yet been contrived by man, by which so much happiness is produced as by a good tavern or inn'.

Dr Samuel Johnson, as reported by his biographer, James Boswell

The earliest known inn signs were used by the Romans to advertise inns and their wares. When the sites of Pompeii and Herculaneum were excavated it was noted that signs placed above or by the side of a door included vine leaves, symbolic of Bacchus, God of Wine, and a bush to indicate a first vintage. This led to the phrase 'a good wine needs no bush'. Sketches outside houses in Pompeii of chequer boards, indicate that board games could be played within. The Latin term, *taverna*, indicated that the establishment provided food, drink, entertainment and lodging. These customs were presumably transported to Roman Britain.

In Anglo-Saxon England the term 'tavern' continued although it seems to have been applied to a mere drinking house, which used the sign of the bush attached to a projecting pole or even a broom, as indicated in scenes from medieval manuscripts. The Anglo Saxons preferred the word 'alehouse' to relate to a drinking establishment and these were controlled by a succession of laws. Three of the oldest inns dating from this period (though it is not clear whether a name was attached to the inn at that time) appear to be the Bingley Arms, Bardsley, which claims to date from AD 905, Ye Olde Fighting Cocks at St Albans, which has an eleventh-century structure on an eighth-century site and the Eagle and Child, Stow on the Wold, which is said to date from AD 947. Later, when ale began to be brewed with hops this drink became beer and was sold in beer-houses. By 1550 almost all ale was brewed with hops and such titles as alehouse, tavern and beer-house were used indiscriminately.

During the medieval period the monasteries provided hospitality both in food, drink and lodging. For the many pilgrims who visited shrines, guesthouses were provided in the monasteries or inns established at or near the entrance. These had to display a pictorial sign as many people could not read and the signs were a means of identification. These included the Old Bell at Malmesbury, Wiltshire, established in 1220, and the George Inn in the village of Norton St Philip, Somerset, which was provided by the Carthusian monks at Hinton Charterhouse in 1397. By the mid-fifteenth century the number of pilgrims visiting Glastonbury Abbey, Somerset, was so great that Abbot John de Selwood in 1470 decided to build an inn at the gate. This, once the George and Pilgrim, survives today as the George.

Many signs had a religious origin. The Star was the star of Bethlehem; the Bull might be the papal *bulla* or a sealed document; the Cross Keys were those held by St Peter, while the Salutation showed the visit of the Angel Gabriel to Mary. The Crusaders added the Saracen's Head and the Turk's Head. Other signs indicate drinking establishments loyal to the Crown or the local nobility. The Red Lion was the badge of John of Gaunt, the Bear and Ragged Staff that of the Earls of Warwick. Some inns put up the coat of arms of the landowner. Other inns merely had long stakes of wood, which were used to stir their brew. These were known as billets and hence the sign of the Crooked Billet.

In 1393 publicans had been compelled by law to display a sign outside their premises: 'whoever shall brew ale in this town with the intention of selling it, must hang out a sign; otherwise he shall forfeit his role'. The result was a huge increase in the number of named inns. In some parts of England an ale-garland (a garland of flowers) had to be hung outside the house to indicate a new brew of beer being offered for sale. Before it could go on sale it had to be tested by official ale-tasters to ensure its strength and taste and that it was being sold at the correct price. The ale-tasters at Congleton, Cheshire, ensured that the ale was of the correct quality by spilling some on benches and sitting on it. If their leather breeches stuck to the bench the ale was deemed to be of suitable quality to be sold.

During the fifteenth century livery companies formed guilds; the Vintners in 1346, the Coopers in 1396 and the Brewers in 1437. All these allowed inns to incorporate their coats of arms or a motif to indicate their wares. The Innholders' Guild was relatively late, being granted its charter in 1515, but it had been founded in the fourteenth century and had been given guild status in London in 1446. The government, however, determined to control places where drink was sold, in 1495, in the reign of Henry VII, gave local magistrates power to license or close alehouses, beer-houses, inns or taverns, that is all public houses or pubs.

At the Reformation, when Henry VIII broke with the Catholic Church, the monasteries were dissolved. There were three results of this. First more inns had to be established to provide the hospitality once given by the monasteries. Secondly to ensure good behaviour, inns were to be licensed by two magistrates who would issue licences each year. Thirdly religious inn signs were now rigidly taboo. The Pope's Head became the King's Head, the Salutation became the Angel and the St John the Baptist became the Lamb and Flag.

So rapidly did the number of inns increase that in the reign of Edward VI an attempt was made to control the number which a town should be allowed. A statute of 1552 reiterated that two Justices of the Peace must license all alehouses yearly: only forty were allowed, for example, in the City of London and eight in York. In the reign of James I an attempt was made at a definition: 'the ancient and principal use of inns and victualling houses is for the receipt, relief and lodging of wayfaring people travelling from place to place'. In practice this distinction was blurred because although many inns did not provide lodgings, all inns sold alcohol of some sort.

The number of inns did decrease during the Puritan Revolution (1649-60), especially 1655-58 when Cromwell divided England into eleven districts placing a Major General at the head of each. Many inns were closed as licences were abolished and those inns that remained were quick to change their signs to suit the new regime. But when Charles II was restored to the throne in 1660 there was an outburst of royalist fervour. Signs were quickly erected indicating loyalty to the Crown (The King's Arms) or commemorating Charles' escape after the Battle of Worcester (The Royal Oak).

In the next century more inns were built. Their signs also became larger. Gallows signs, which are those stretching across the road, were intended to attract travellers. William Harrison, in his description of England written in 1677, says that some signs cost £30 to £40, a considerable sum in those times, for what was a 'meere vanity'. As early as 1419, the Lord Mayor and Aldermen of London, alarmed at the size of the signs, had decreed that no sign over the King's Highway should be more than 7ft long. That this was routinely ignored was noted in a tragedy, which occurred in 1718 when a huge sign in Fleet Street in London was so heavy that it fell down, bringing the front of the inn with it and killing two passers-by. It was not until 1797, however, that it was decreed that no sign should project in any way to be a nuisance and seemingly this was observed.

Admiral Rodney, Prestbury.

Improvements in transport led to more inns being built and more variety in inn signs. Coaching inns put up signs such as the Coach and Horses. The development of canals resulted in inns being built by the side of locks and improvements in shipping resulted in inns being provided at harbours and docks. But it was the development of the railways that had the greatest impact and there were few towns that did not have a Railway Inn. Railway mania meant that many publicans changed their signs. This proliferation of inns, pubs and other drinking establishments meant that there was hardly a subject which was not represented at some time. Trade, banking, military matters, flora and fauna, historic events, myths, legends and local and national characters all made an appearance.

Loyalty to the crown intensified during Victoria's long reign, when a large number of pubs were built or rebuilt, often being called The Victoria, The Queen or Queen Victoria, to take advantage of an increase in the drinking population. Many had two bars, the public bar where the working class drank and a saloon, where the foremen, mill owners and the gentry congregated. Drinks were, of course priced higher in the saloon. Other social distinctions, especially in industrial towns, were preserved by a 'jug and bottle', a ladies wine bar and a private bar. Although women had used inns during the coaching era, they ceased to be welcomed in many pubs, possibly because pubs in working-class areas became the preserve of men. Class distinctions in the nineteenth century meant that middle- and upper-class women avoided being seen there. During the Second World War, when class distinctions began to break down, women began to frequent pubs. Even so, separation of the bars was often kept until the 1960s and then they were removed by the simple expedient of taking down partitions, but many pubs still have two rooms, a public and a saloon.

It was at the end of the twentieth century that the number of pubs began to decrease as breweries amalgamated or closed them, becoming private houses or being demolished to provide a building site. Chains of pubs preferred to have the same logo for every one of their establishments so that the local name was abandoned or the pictorial sign removed in favour of a name or a device so that, for example, the sign of a coat of arms was replaced by the name of the family. The Albert might become just PA on a black background; the coat of arms of the Tollemache family was replaced by their name. This is regrettable as signs are part of a long tradition and also give enormous pleasure to passers-by. It is a reminder of Hilaire Belloc's comment, 'When you have lost your inn, drown your empty selves, for you will have lost the last of England'.

Nevertheless there still remain a large number of signs that do reflect the history of the area or have a local and possibly sentimental meaning. Some brewers have an excellent policy for keeping and repainting inn signs, even if they give a modern twist to what was a serious subject. They deserve our gratitude for keeping up the ancient tradition. Given these developments, it is essential that signs should be recorded before they disappear entirely from the local scene.

A–Z OF CHESHIRE INN SIGNS

A

ABBEY ARMS, Delamere. This was once the courthouse where the magistrates met to determine the licences for the public houses in the area. Above the door is the coat of arms of the former abbey: the three lions of England bisected by a crosier and set within a bordure. Edward I had founded an abbey for Cistercian monks, before he became King, in fulfilment of a vow he had made when he was in danger of shipwreck when crossing the English Channel. This was probably in the winter of 1263-64. The first site chosen was not satisfactory and the abbey was re-sited at Vale Royal before Edward's campaign against Wales in 1278. The abbey was dissolved at the Reformation and the land became part of the Cholmondley estates.

ADMIRAL RODNEY, Prestbury. The inn sign portrays George Brydges, Admiral Lord Rodney (1718-92). He distinguished himself by capturing Martinique in 1762 during the Seven Years War and defeating a French and Spanish fleet at the Battle of the Saints in 1782 in the Caribbean, which secured the island of Jamaica for the British Crown. (*See* **Lord Rodney**.)

THE ALBERT, various locations. Prince Francis Albert Augustus Charles Emmanuel (1819-61), the second son of Ernest, Duke of Saxe-Coburg-Gotha, married Queen Victoria in 1840 and was created Prince Consort in 1857. He tried to take a more active interest in politics than the British Government thought was appropriate and became very unpopular. After his help in the creation of the Great Exhibition in 1851 his popularity increased and he was instrumental in securing funds to create the group of museums dedicated to arts and sciences in South Kensington. His memorial is situated on the south side of Hyde Park. Albert and Prince Albert became popular names for pubs during the late-nineteenth century. Many pubs such as **The Albert Hotel** at Widnes display a sign of the Prince in military uniform and have kept most of their original features.

ALBION INN, Chester, which faces the city walls, was built in 1715 but now promotes a Victorian atmosphere with William Morris wallpaper, enamel advertisements and cast-iron fireplaces and tables. It also has a First World War theme with memorabilia of newspapers, signs and portraits, as well as four officially listed war memorials. Many of the artefacts were rescued from a nearby skip. There is a patriotic sign over the door: six union flags surround the name Albion Inn with the words Rule Britannia beneath. **The Albion**, Macclesfield, has a sign portraying the British Isles in black on a white background, which refers to a poetic name for Britain, (Latin: albus or white), possibly a reference to the whiteness of the cliffs of Dover. **The Albion Hotel**, Widnes, has a sign showing the British flag triumphantly flying above a harbour. (*See* **British Flag**.)

ALSAGER ARMS, Alsager. The sign depicts the arms of the Alsager family, ermine, in chief three gold lions rampant, with a squirrel as a crest. The family were established in the area by AD 1250 and gave their name to the village, which is now a small town. The Loyal Order of Shepherds used the pub as a meeting place in the nineteenth century.

ALVANLEY ARMS, Cotebrook, Little Budworth. This was first built in the 1660s as a coaching inn. At one time it was a centre for cockfighting. The interior contains pictures of the Cheshire Hunt, bridles, horse brasses, rosettes and halters as well as pictures of shire horses identifying it with the nearby Shire Horse Centre.

ANCHOR, various locations. The name is to be found near canals for its obvious nautical connection, though the anchor would be most likely to be dug into the canal bank than dropped in the canal. It sometimes had religious connections, as the anchor was a sign of hope based on the words of St Paul 'which hope we have for an anchor of the soul both sure and steadfast' (Hebrews 6:19). **The Anchor**, Lymm, was converted from a former tollhouse to a coaching inn in the eighteenth century. It has a nautical theme based on the Battle of Trafalgar.

ANGEL. The name has religious connotations as the sign depicted the visitation of the Angel Gabriel to the Virgin Mary. After the Reformation it fell out of favour but the figure of the angel was kept. **The Angel**, Knutsford, an eighteenth-century pub, with an ornate canopy over the door, has a most suitable sign. This is in the form of a stained glass window, with an angel in white, sitting beneath a Gothic arch and playing a musical instrument

THE ANTELOPE, Congleton. The sign often derives from distorted pictures of the White Hart, which was the badge of Richard II, Henry IV, Henry V, Henry VI and Edward IV. The sign on this pub straightforwardly shows an African antelope with large twisted horns while the wide African veldt stretches behind it.

ANTROBUS ARMS, Antrobus. This 200-year-old pub was formerly called The Wheatsheaf and still keeps a wheatsheaf on its sign, but the name was changed to commemorate an old Cheshire family. The pub is the centre for the Antrobus Soulers

The Angel, Knutsford. *The Antelope, Congleton.*

who parade on All Souls' Day (2 November) around various pubs in the area and perform a ritual play, which is said to date back several hundred years.

APPLETON ARMS, Widnes. The sign is a heraldic one showing a blue shield with three white apples on it surrounded by blue and white mantling.

THE ARK, Winsford. The sign shows the typical view of Noah's ark with the animals approaching it in twos. The giraffes and the polar bears are prominent. Birds line the roof and the family are to be seen on the deck.

ASH TREE, Disley. This was a coaching inn in the eighteenth century.

B

BADGER INN, Church Minshall. This fifteenth-century inn, once a coaching inn on the Nantwich to Middlewich run, was originally the Brookes Arms, named after the family who lived at Norton Priory and who owned land in this area. The wrought-iron sign, although showing badgers is a play on words, for Brookes (the family name) may also be 'brock', the nickname of a badger, so that a badger is part of the family crest. Opposite to the pub is Church Farm, once the home of Elizabeth Minshall who married the poet, John Milton. This is yet another pub threatened with closure.

BARGE, Runcorn. The sign is suitable for this former farmhouse situated on the canal bank.

BARLEY MOW, various locations. A mow is a stack and barley is an ingredient of beer so the sign could indicate that beer was sold in the pub. **The Barley Mow**, Warrington, a half-timbered house dating to 1561, is now situated in the middle of a shopping centre. The sign shows two farm workers hoisting hay onto a waggon. Within the pub is a Jacobean-style chimneypiece and an eighteenth-century staircase. In 1838 it was sold to a Mr J. Hepherd and remained in the hands of that family until 1919. Since then, members of the family are reputed to haunt the pub. **The Barley Mow**, Runcorn, a Victorian pub, has the motif etched on the windows.

THE BARN OWL INN, Lymm, with its sign of an owl perched on a tree stump, was formerly a boatyard building at Agden Wharf situated by the Bridgwater Canal.

BASSET HOUND, Heswall. The name comes from a thirteenth-century lord of the manor of Thirlwall, Sir Ralph Basset, who fought besides Simon De Montfort at the Battle of Evesham (1265). A basset hound is also a hunting dog. The lounges in this pub are called Kennel and Doghouse and are decorated with hunting horns and horse brasses.

THE BATE HALL, Macclesfield. The pub is on the site of the original town house of the Stopford family. The sign shows the arms of the Earls of Courtown: azure; three lozenges or between three crosses crosslets of the last, crest; a wyvern, wings displayed vert, supporters; two stags rampant, collared and chained. This, the oldest coaching inn in Macclesfield, is said to date from 1525. In 1557 it was known to be the home of the mayor, Humphrey Bate. It still retains the original Jacobean stairs and a priest's hole. The Courtown connection comes with the fact that it was the town house of the Stopford family. James Stopford had fought with the Parliamentary army in Ireland in 1641 and acquired land there. His grandson was created Baron Courtown in 1738 and Earl of Courtown and Viscount Stopford in 1762. His son James, who held land in Saltersford in Macclesfield forest, reported to be 'the most dreary part of a mountainous district', was created Baron Stopford of Saltersford and used a rebuilt Bate Hall as a town house in Macclesfield. The building was converted to a public house in the early nineteenth century.

BEAR & BILLET, Chester. The sign shows a bear clutching a staff or a billet in its left paw and a tankard of ale in its right. The name is said to come from the action of Russian sailors who, when billeted at the inn, left their ships guarded by bears, but the name may equally be a variant of the Bear and Ragged Staff because a billet is a log of wood, although this was sometimes used as a weapon. The date inscribed on the front is 1664 but part of the inn is of an earlier date and some timbers are said to be from Armada ships which sought refuge at Chester when making their way round the north of Britain after being defeated in the Channel in 1588. Charles I is said to have jumped from an upper window into a cart stationed below to avoid being made prisoner when he was holed up in Chester before the Battle of Rowton Moor in 1645. On the upper storey are the folding doors of the granary into which corn and provisions for the family were hoisted and stored. It was originally the home of the Sergeants of the Bridge Gate, an official title held by the Earls of Shrewsbury, who, with their family and retainers, used it as a town house when he was in Chester. It has been an inn since the eighteenth century and with its panelled walls and uneven floors has great charm.

BEAR AND RAGGED STAFF, Tattenhall. The sign is drawn on a side wall. The pub is said to have got its name from the fact that the Earl of Warwick stayed there when boar hunting. The bear and ragged staff was adopted as the badge of the Neville family, the Earls of Warwick and their retainers. Arthgal, the first earl was called The Bear because he was reputed to have strangled that animal. A later ancestor was said to have slain a giant with a club, which he tore off a young tree, hence the staff. Shakespeare mentioned the badge in (*Henry VI* Part II, Act 5 Sc 1), when Warwick says:

> Now, by my father's badge, old Nevil's crest,
> The rampant bear chain'd to the ragged staff;
> This day I'll wear aloft my burgonet.

Above: *Bear and Ragged Staff, Tattenhall.*

Right: *Bear & Billet, Chester.*

Bears Head, Brereton Green.

The bear and staff would appear on his shield; the burgonet was a helmet. The sign is now sketched on the wall of the pub, which is mainly a Thai restaurant.

BEARS HEAD, various locations. The bear is particularly associated with Cheshire, partly because of the county's devotion to bear-baiting, which was banned in 1835. It was also the crest of the Brereton family who played a significant role in Cheshire history. At Brereton Green this former coaching inn on the busy Liverpool to London route, built about 1615, was called the **Bears Head** in 1788. Two years later it became the Boars Head, but by 1822 had reverted to its much more appropriate name. The local legend states that in the sixteenth century, Sir William Brereton murdered his valet. He was imprisoned and was challenged to design a muzzle, which would effectively fit on a bear, which presumably would attack him. He quickly completed the muzzle, which defeated a bear released to attack him, and from then on incorporated a bear's head as a crest on the family coat of arms. This pub sign was originally a fearsome bear's head but has recently been replaced by a cartoon bear, with a very self-satisfied smirk.

THE BEARS PAW, Frodsham, a former coaching inn, once had its own boathouse and mooring. It dates from 1632 and was a centre for bear-baiting. The pub was known as the Bears Paw and Posting Office when it collected the mail in the eighteenth century. When the railway arrived it became the Bears Paw and Railway Hotel. It has now reverted to the Bears Paw. The arms purport to be those of the Savage family, the name

Beeston Castle, Beeston.   *Bears Paw, Frodsham.*

of the Earls Rivers, lords of the manor of Frodsham, with supporters of a unicorn and a falcon. The peerage became extinct in 1728. The crest is said to be a bear's paw, which would ally to the name of the inn, but it may have been confused with the correct crest which is a lion's gamb (forepaw) erect. The motto is *a te, pro te* (from you, for you). Inside is a panel showing a piece of the original wattle and daub. There are oak beams and low ceilings.

THE BEARTOWN TAP, Congleton. This pub was originally The Grapes Tavern, then the Grapevine. It now is an outlet for beer from the Beartown Brewery and has two bears on its sign. The name refers to the fact that Congleton is nicknamed 'Beartown'. Bear-baiting was very popular in Congleton but a crisis arose in the 1660s when the town bear died just before the Wakes holiday. Allegedly, rather than face resentful townspeople, the town corporation is said to have sold the town's Bible to buy a new bear. A less disreputable story is that they borrowed money to buy a new bear from that saved in the parish chest for the purchase of a new Bible.

THE BEESTON CASTLE at Beeston, with its sign of a representation of Beeston Castle and the approach bridge, was formerly the Tollemache Arms. Lord Tollemache commanded that trains should stop outside the pub to allow travellers to obtain victuals at his hotel. (*See* **Dysart Arms**.) In the nineteenth century it was the hostelry patronised by farmers who sold their cattle at the nearby market. It is now a cosy pub with log fires and numerous pictures and horse brasses.

BELLS OF PEOVER, Lower Peover. The building is said to be at least 700 years old. Originally it was called the Warren de Tabley Arms but changed its name when the Bell family took it over. It was also known as the Brewery when one of the Bells married a Mobberley woman who bought the recipe for brewing. George Bell brewed beer for thirty years until, in 1871, he went to Hillsborough Castle in Ireland. At the birth of the 6th Marquis of Devonshire he made a special brew, which in 1892 was tapped on the heir's twenty-first birthday for 4,000 people to drink. During the Second World War the pub was used by the American Third Army, which was stationed in the area before moving to the south coast to take part in the D-Day landings. Generals Eisenhower and Patton were billeted in Over Peover Hall and worshipped in Over Peover church, They also made use of the pub and General Patton gave permission for the Stars and Stripes to be flown at the pub so that to this day American and British flags fly outside the building.

BHURTPORE INN, Aston. The pub contains a collection of artefacts with an Indian theme. This is not surprising as can be explained by the sign. One side of the sign shows Sir Stapleton Cotton dressed in regimental uniform and on the other an Indian Sepoy in brown uniform and turban holding a rifle and fixed bayonet. The name commemorates the taking by British troops of Bhurtpore, an Indian city in January 1826. The Commander in Chief of the British forces in India from 1825 was Sir Stapleton Cotton (1773-1865), a local Cheshire landowner. He had been created Baron Combermere of Combermere in 1814 in recognition of his distinguished service in the Peninsular War, when Wellington defeated the French forces. In 1827, as further recognition of the capture of Bhurtpore he was created Viscount Combermere. During his distinguished Army career he was raised to the rank of field marshall in 1855 and became Constable of the Tower of London. In recognition of his action when he led the decisive charge but was badly wounded at the Battle of Salamanca in 1812, he founded two inns. Unfortunately **The Salamanca** at Wrenbury is now a private house and **The Salamanca** at Smallwood has now been demolished. (*See* **Combermere Arms**.)

BICKERTON POACHER, Broxton. This pub was originally called the Red Lion. When this pub was sold in 1761 it changed hands at £63 10s. and in 1877 it was sold for £1,160. The sign showing a poacher was unfortunately lost in a fire several years ago. The pub is now a popular stop on the Sandstone Trail.

BIG LOCK, Middlewich. The nearby lock suffices for the name. This pub is built as a stack construction, with a main entrance from the street at ground floor level. There was a separate entrance under the ground floor, level with the canal, until the 1970s, which was originally made for the bargemen to enter. The pub had a chandler's shop and the name relates to Lock 75 on the adjoining Trent and Mersey Canal. Attached was a stable block with a hay store above, which has now been incorporated into the public rooms.

Bird in Hand, Mobberley.

BIRD IN HAND, Mobberley. There is a popular saying, 'A bird in the hand is worth two in the bush' meaning possession is better than expectation, which may be the origin of this sign. The saying occurs in many different languages. It also refers to the art of falconry and the Mobberley sign of this late-eighteenth-century pub, is a traditional one showing a falcon perched while tethered on a leather glove.

BLACK BEAR, Warrington. This developed as an early coaching inn and the sign shows an amicable bear. The **Black Bear**, Chester, occupies one of the oldest buildings in the city being built in 1670. (*See* **Bears Head**.)

THE BLACK DOG, Waverton. The sign depicts a black labrador seated on its haunches. The Black Dog of Arden was the nickname given to Guy de Beauchamp, Earl of Warwick (1272-1315). The Earls of Warwick had some connection with Cheshire (*See* **Bear and Ragged Staff**), but dogs, especially labradors, are also great companions and are often part of the family.

BLACK LION, various locations. It was the heraldic device of Philippa of Hainault, who came from Flanders to marry Edward III, and also of Owen Glendower (Owain Glyndwr *c.* 1359-*c.* 1416), a Welsh chieftain who led a series of revolts against Henry IV in the early fifteenth century. The fact that Cheshire adjoins Wales may be the reason for the name of **The Black Lion** in Nantwich, which is a former coaching inn dating to 1664.

The Black Dog, Waverton.

BLACK SWAN, Lower Withington. A black swan is the emblem of Western Australia, but this may be a far-fetched explanation of the origin of the sign of this eighteenth-century coaching inn, which is nicknamed The Trap by locals as it is situated on Trap Street. The Roman poet Juvenal (*Satires* 6. 1. 65) considered the black swan to be a rare bird (*rara avis in terris nigroque simillima cygne*) i.e. 'a rare bird on this earth, like nothing so much as the black swan'. It is suggested that its appearance on pub signs indicated what a rare bird a certain landlord was. **The Black Swan**, Hollins Green, is a former eighteenth-century coaching inn

THE BLACKSMITHS ARMS, Henbury. The pub is a very large and rebuilt extension of the original smithy. The former blacksmith's forge was incorporated as a dining room. A 3-D sign shows in the upper part a blacksmith leaning on his arms, hammer in one hand, tongs in the other.

BLEEDING WOLF, Scholar Green. This is a thatched pub, which has twice been saved from disastrous fires which started in the thatched roof. There was originally a pub located next to the road where the car park is now situated. The present sign shows a wolf standing on a cliff's edge in the snow, head turned to lick its wounds. The name is confined to Cheshire. The usual explanation is that the name indicated the crest of Hugh D'Avranche, 1st Earl of Chester, nicknamed Lupus (the Wolf), which was a wolf's head torn from its body. Sign painters elaborated beyond the head to show the whole body of a wolf with blood dripping from its sides. Another explanation is that

Bleeding Wolf, Scholar Green.

it relates to the legend that the last wolf in England was killed in Macclesfield Forest in 1746. Yet another, detailed in the inn and depicted in a painting, relates to a legend regarding King John (1198-1216). When John was hunting in the forest a wolf sprang at him. His horse bolted throwing the King to the ground. Luckily a keeper of the forest was nearby and thrust his knife into the wolf, blood streaming from the gaping wound. Recognising the King, the keeper fell to his knees but was ordered to rise. He was told that, taking the corpse of the wolf as his starting point, he could have all the land he could walk over in a week. This he did thus founding the estate of Lawton, his own name. To commemorate his possession of the land, he built an inn on the spot where he had killed the wolf.

BLUE BARREL, Northwich. Although the building is modern it stands on part of the *vicus* (the civilian area) attached to the Roman fort. It is suggested that the earliest building on the site dates from the time of the Civil War as the first-known landlord was mentioned in 1644. This was the date of the Battle of Nantwich when the Parliamentary forces defeated those of Charles I.

BLUE BELL, various locations. The **Blue Bell**, Tushington, dates in part from 1667 and is said to be haunted by a duck, probably a unique claim. The **Blue Bell**, Smallwood, has a blue painted bell placed above the sign. The list of publicans goes back to Thomas Gibson in 1763.

BLUE CAP, Cuddington. This is named after a greyhound, portrayed on the sign, which won several races in the eighteenth century. The Honourable J. Barry of Marbury Hall owned it and when Blue Cap died he was buried in the pub garden. The gravestone cannot be seen now as it was moved to the kennels of the Cheshire Hunt in the 1950s.

BOAR'S HEAD, various locations. The boar's head, served with an apple or a lemon in its mouth, was a welcome addition to a Christmas feast. The Queen's College, Oxford, continues the tradition, and sing the sixteenth-century Boar's Head carol as a boar's head is processed into the hall. The **Boar's Head**, Poynton, with its sign of a fearsomely tusked boar, was built in 1904 to replace an earlier pub frequented by miners who worked in the Poynton coalmines. The Anson Mine dug 1,000 tons a day using 150 men. Boats on the Macclesfield Canal transported the coal until the mine closed in 1926. The **Boar's Head,** Walgherton, is said to date back to 1534. In the porch is a fine painting of a boar's head.

THE BOARHOUND, Macclesfield, has a sign with the head and shoulders of this animal gazing sternly at the viewer. Boarhounds were especially bred for hunting.

BOATHOUSE, Chester. This pub was originally a boathouse, which once incorporated two pubs, the Dee (public bar), and the River Bar (lounge). The Dee has now closed. Decoration included old paddles, pictures of the River Dee and beer bottles. The lounge once had porthole windows, which overlooked the river. Wide ocean liner ones have replaced these, giving a splendid view of the river.

BOOT & SHOE, Nantwich. The sign displays a boot and a high-heeled red shoe and below a shoemaker's hammer. Parts of the building survived the 1583 fire but the front wall is obviously a brick rebuild of the nineteenth century.

BOROUGH ARMS, Crewe. The pub was built about 1867 as a beer-house to serve railway workers. The sign is devised as a shield divided quarterly: top left, a canal barge; top right a stage coach; lower left, a groom holding a horse; lower right, two people riding one horse. Below is a motto: Never Behind.

BOWLING GREEN, Leftwich. This probably was once a farmhouse and is one of the oldest buildings in the Northwich area. There is a date of 1650 on part of the building but close scrutiny will reveal that this particular part of the building is not of seventeenth-century date. It is an extension of 1938. The date of 1650 over the door is probably correct for that part of the farmhouse building. **The Bowling Green**, Northwich. This pub is next to the Salt Museum. The building dates from 1650 but only traded as licensed premises from 1763. The name comes from a bowling green that was situated at the rear and was one of the few L-shaped ones. This dated from 1777 and was said to have caused problems for the bowlers.

THE BREWERS ARMS, Macclesfield. The sign shows a publican, holding a tankard after preparing a brew. The **Brewers Arms**, Neston, has a punning sign of a shield showing a chevron on which are three tuns. Above and below are crossed wheat sheaves; the crest is a helmet surmounted by a child.

BRIDGE INN, Audlem. The pub, quite logically, is situated near a bridge by the canal and has a sign of a barge going under the bridge. When it was built in the 1830s, it was known as the Canal Tavern. The **Bridge Inn**, Burtonwood. The sign shows a bridge with a horse walking under it. The pub was near a bridge, which crossed a stream running through the village. The **Bridge Hotel**, Prestbury has a sign showing a bridge over the river, which flows by its side.

THE BRIDGEWATER ARMS, Macclesfield. The sign shows a barge passing under a roving bridge on the Macclesfield Canal. Francis Egerton, 3rd Duke of Bridgewater (1738-1803), began the development of the canal system in England by having a canal cut to convey coal from his Worsley estate to Manchester. Later, in 1772, the canal was extended to the River Mersey thus providing a water route connecting Manchester and Liverpool. The pub is near the Macclesfield Marina on the Macclesfield Canal, a popular boating canal, which is part of the Cheshire Ring.

BRIGHTON BELLE, Winsford. This was originally the Railway Inn but changed its name when a former railway carriage, which plied the London to Brighton line and was used as a dining room, was placed by its side. This carriage was removed in the 1990s when the Brighton Belle was refurbished, but the name of the pub has remained. The sign displays a very demure young lady seated in a restaurant car, presumably that of the Brighton Belle, being eyed speculatively by an elderly gentleman.

BRITANNIA INN, Hurdsfield. The Romans first gave the name Britannia to their Roman province and depicted a seated woman with helmet, spear and shield on their coins. The model for the present figure of Britannia was Frances Stuart, Duchess of Richmond, one of Charles II's many mistresses. The inn sign shows a seated Britannia on a rock in the traditional pose with helmet, trident and a shield painted with the Union Jack.

BRITISH FLAG, Macclesfield. The landlord has a collection of memorabilia and trophies of Macclesfield Football Club. The pub was originally a ginger beer brewery. It has a sign showing the Union Jack blowing in the wind and in addition flies the flag on a pole above the roof. The pub is quite accurate its nomenclature as the British Flag is the correct name. When James VI of Scotland succeeded to the English throne as James I of England in 1603, there was a problem about flying the correct flag on ships, whether it should be the Scottish or the English flag. In 1606 it was decreed that all ships should fly the British Flag comprising the cross of St George and the cross

The British Lion, Crewe.

of St Andrew conjoined. There were several variants of this design but it lasted until 1801 when, on Ireland being incorporated in Britain, the flag integrated the cross of St Patrick. The flag is commonly called the Union Jack but strictly speaking this term should only be used when the flag is flown on the bow of HM ships. A government announcement, however, made in the House of Lords in 1908, said that the Union Jack should be regarded as the national flag.

THE BRITISH LION, Crewe. This pub has the proud sign of a gold lion rampant, with a crown above its head. A lion has always been incorporated into the coat of arms of the English Kings and has come to represent the English/British nation.

BROWN HORSE, Neston. This eighteenth-century pub in the centre of Neston with its pictures of old Wirral has the sign appropriate to its name.

BROWNLOW INN, Astbury. The pub was built in the nineteenth century and has since been extended. Although it is named after the area, it has the coat of arms of Baron Brownlow as its sign: ermine, on a chevron sable, three fountains; crest, a lion's head erased, sable, collared or paly wavy of six argent and azure. There are two lions as supporters. The motto is *esse quam videri* (to be rather than to seem).

BRUNEL ARMS, Crewe. The pub displays a shield with a medieval ship on it; above is a helm with two laurel leaves as a crest.

Bull & Stirrup, Chester.

BRUNSWICK ARMS, Crewe. This is a small pub built to serve railway workers at the nearby station. The sign shows a shield with two gold lions couchant on a red shield. The crest is a ducal coronet.

BULL & STIRRUP, Chester. This is a large Victorian pub with a sign of a bull above a shield from which dangles a stirrup. In the lobby of the side entrance is a mosaic, which is labelled 'Edgar the Pacific being rowed along the River Dee by eight tributary princes'. This commemorates an historic incident. Edgar became King of Wessex in AD 959. He was crowned at Winchester in 973 and soon after came to Chester. According to a West Midland annalist, known as Florence of Worcester, while Edgar held the rudder, he was rowed on the Dee to the church of St John and back, by Kenneth, King of Scots, Malcolm, King of the Cumbrians, Maccus, 'King of many islands', and five other princes named as Dufnal, Siferth, Huwal, Jacob and Juchil, after they had sworn fealty to him. The rowing was probably a symbolic act by which these princes expressed their subjection to their lord. It is most curious that the incident is commemorated in this Chester pub.

BULLS HEAD, various locations. The original pub sign of a seal (Latin – *bulla*) became unpopular after the Reformation as it was associated with papal seals on documents. It quickly became transformed into the head of the animal. This very common sign in Cheshire is appropriate as it is a farming county. The sign also has heraldic importance appearing in the arms of the Worshipful Company of Butchers. The **Bulls Head** at Clotton was a stopping place for farmers who called here on their way to Beeston

Bulls Head, Lymm.

market. Many pubs, such as the **Bulls Head** in Congleton, which, until recently, did not have a sign, and now has one displaying an outline sketch of a bull's head, and the **Bulls Head** at Davenham, built in 1764, with its modern sign, were originally coaching inns. Licensees of the **Bulls Head** in Congleton until the end of the nineteenth century had the right to have a pew in the town church of St Peter. The sixteenth-century **Bulls Head** at Lymm is situated by Lymm Bridge on the Shropshire Union Canal. Like most of the signs the bull has a ring in its nose.

C

CABBAGE HALL, Little Budworth. The sign depicts Thomas Walker, a Manchester tailor, who ran a tailor's shop and pub in the nineteenth century. Cabbage is slang for the spare cut-off cloth, which he saved when he was making clothes. The profit from this enabled him to keep the pub.

CARDEN ARMS, Tilston. This was a coaching inn, first licensed in the early seventeenth century, on the Carden estate. It is reputed to be haunted by the ghost of a lady who

The Castle, Macclesfield.

fell from her horse and broke her neck. The Carden family held a large amount of property in the area from the reign of Richard II (1377-1399). In 1698 the family moved to Ireland and rented Templemore Castle in Co. Kildare on the estate of the Earl of Ormonde, from whom they purchased it in 1701. The inn sign with the family coat of arms and the name is one of the last memories of this local family.

CARRIER'S INN, Hatchmere, Norley. This seventeenth-century pub has a sign displaying two shire horses pulling a heavily laden waggon. One man stands by their heads, another sits on the waggon. The gardens lead down to Hatchmere Lake. The pub is nicknamed the Snig's Foot which is the name of a baby eel.

CASTLE, various locations. Most signs display some form of castle. **The Castle**, Macclesfield, stands on the site of the gatehouse of a house founded by John de Legh, later John de Macclesfield, recorded as the mayor 1358-59. Later he petitioned Richard II for a licence to embattle and crenellate his house. A stone bearing the date 1400 is built into the wall of the passage called Palace Yard, which may be the date when a fortified manor house was completed. The remains of the building were demolished in 1933. Part of the original masonry can be seen in Palace Yard and also in Back Wallgate. A few stones are preserved in the Town Hall courtyard. The key kept behind the bar is said to be one of the original keys. The sign depicts the inner courtyard of a castle with a knight and lady on the left, and on the right, a file of peasants walking to take up their jobs. In the foreground a man rolls out a bolt of cloth. **The Castle**, Halton. The original castle was built on the site of an Anglo-Saxon stronghold probably because of its superb view overlooking the Mersey. It was the stronghold of the hereditary Constables of Chester, Barons of Halton. In 1311 it passed by marriage to the Duchy of Lancaster and later, in the reign of Henry IV, came into the possession of the Crown. It played an important part in northern history as it commanded a crossing of the River Mersey. After the Civil War it was dismantled and some of its stones were used in the present building on the site of the original gatehouse, which became the Duchy of Lancaster Court House. The cellar, which is said to be haunted, once contained cells of the prison. Over the door is the Hanoverian coat of arms of George III. There is a splendid view from behind the building over the River Mersey. The sign at the **Castle Inn**, Congleton depicts a castle akin to Harlech Castle in Wales.

THE CAT, Ellesmere Port. The sign depicts a large cat resting on the branch of a tree. This, however, is a large wild cat – a leopard.

THE CAT & FIDDLE, Wildboarclough. The highest inn in England is Tan Hill Inn on Stainmoor, Yorkshire at a height of 1,732ft (528m). The second highest inn is the **Cat & Fiddle** situated at 1,690ft (515m) on the winding road between Macclesfield and Buxton. In wintry weather it can be isolated and the road, with its twists and turns, has been named as the most dangerous in the United Kingdom. This is a very popular pub and the road is a constant attraction for motorcyclists who sweep along it to make the **Cat & Fiddle** a central meeting point. The sign has been changed several times but it always depicts the cat and a fiddle. The present one displays a cat, standing on sheets of music, glowering over a fiddle. There is, however, a stone carving of a cat playing a fiddle, which constantly stares out at any outside drinkers. There are several theories as to the origin of the name. One is that the strings of a fiddle are made from a cat's entrails, so that a small fiddle is called a kit (kitten). The name could be a corruption of the French term, *le chat fidèle* (the faithful cat); it might be a reference to Caton le Fidèle, once Governor of Calais, in the late sixteenth century. This date, however, is too late so it may perhaps be a reference to Catherine la Fidele, a name for Henry VIII's first wife, Catherine of Aragon. The cat and fiddle are immortalised in the very old nursery rhyme, *Hey diddle diddle, the cat and the fiddle*, which dates back at least to the beginning of sixteenth century.

CAT & LION, Stretton. This opened as a pub in 1861 and is now a Premier Inn. It was once owned by the Lyon family, which had the Cheshire cat in its coat of arms. The inn has two signs, showing a cat and a lion, one at the side of the building and the other on a circular painting above the entrance, which has the words:

> The Lion is strong. The Cat is vicious.
> My ale is good and so are my liquors

Above: *Cat & Fiddle, Wildboarclough*.
Right: *Chat Moss Hotel, Glazebury*.

CHAPEL HOUSE, Burtonwood. It once had the nearby church on its sign but now had something like a woodcut of the church, as it might have been in the previous century. It was used as a meeting place and for payment of taxes. A small building at the rear was probably a farrier's establishment.

CHAT MOSS HOTEL, Glazebury, was once George Stevenson's site office and partly served as a railway station on the Liverpool to Manchester line. Tickets were sold in the waiting room. At one time there were benches from the old platforms in the beer garden. To enable the trains to cross Chat Moss, Stevenson put down hurdles made from birch trees interlaced with cotton waste to make a solid foundation. The area now has a market garden industry. Inside the pub are pictures of steam engines. Stevenson and his *Rocket* engine are suitably commemorated on the sign. (*See* also **Railway**.)

CHERRY ORCHARD, Broughton. The pub was named after the Chekhov play.

CHESHIRE CAT, Chistleton. The pub, which has been in operation since 1973, is the former Chistleton Lodge (Innkeepers Lodge) and the building dates from 1801. There are two signs. One shows a cartoon cat, similar to that in the Disney film, *Alice in Wonderland*, grinning from ear to ear, perched on the branch of a tree; the other is of a placid brown cat with a stern stare as if to say that it wishes to enjoy its rest. This is seemingly the only pub named after the Cheshire cat. There was one in Nantwich but this had now closed. There is an old Cheshire saying: 'To grin like a Cheshire polecat'. This was interpreted by Peter Pindar in his *Pair of Lyric Epistles* (1795) as

'Lo, like a Cheshire cat, our court will grin'. One version of the origin of the cat is that local cheeses were fashioned into animal shapes, one being in the form of a grinning cat. Another is that heraldic drawings of lions more often depicted grinning cats. The most famous representative of the Cheshire cat is in Lewis Carroll's *Alice in Wonderland* (1865). 'I didn't know that Cheshire cats always grinned,' said Alice; 'in fact, I didn't know that cats could grin.' 'They all can,' said the Duchess; 'and most of them do'. In the book, Sir John Tenniel illustrated the cat grinning down at Alice from a branch and as Alice watched, the cat 'vanished quite slowly, beginning with the end of the tail, and ending with the grin, which remained for some time after the rest of it had gone'. If the idea that cats in Cheshire grinned because they were so amused by the fact that Cheshire was a County Palatine, that is, not entirely under civil and ecclesiastical government, they had to stop grinning in 1830 when Cheshire lost that right. They might have lamented in 1974 when Cheshire lost the Palatine designation and will positively howl in 2009 when Cheshire is divided into two administrations – East and West Cheshire.

CHESHIRE CHEESE, various locations. Cheshire is famous for its crumbly white and red cheeses, which were first mentioned in Domesday Book. There is also a Blue Cheshire, the bulk of which is produced in Shropshire. Once produced entirely around Chester, from the twelfth century, Cheshire cheese has been made on many farms and is now produced commercially. Its distinctive salty flavour is said to be the result of being made from the milk produced by cows grazing on the salty pastures of Cheshire. George Borrow, however, on a visit to Chester, was scathing about it. (*See* **The Pied Bull**.) The **Cheshire Cheese**, Wheelock, established as an inn in 1863, has a splendid sign of a traditional large cheese round with a slice cut out of it. Others signs are less respectful. **The Cheshire Cheese**, Middlewich, had barges moored on the canal at the back ready to ship the cheeses. These were taken as far as London and the long journey allowed them to mature, thus giving the cheese its special flavour. The sign shows a slice of cheese on which rests a cheeky mouse patting his full stomach, quite unaware than a black cat is creeping towards him. The **Cheshire Cheese**, Nantwich, displays a sign showing a large round of cheese with a slice cut out of it. A mouse, resembling the mouse in the *Tom and Jerry* cartoons, holds a piece of cheese devouring it with great satisfaction. The **Cheshire Cheese**, Frodsham, is another pub with a mouse on its sign. This is a well-fed mouse, with a large round stomach, resting against a cheese, with a contented smile on its face. By the side of the cheese is an empty glass pint beer pot.

THE CHESHIRE TAVERN, Congleton, which was previously called by the innocuous name of the Woodlands, now displays a splendid sign of the former arms of the county of Cheshire: three garbs and sword with the crest of a lion and a feather, and two lions holding feathers as supporters. The shield, however, should be blue rather than green. The motto, *jure et dignitate gladii,* (by the right and power of the sword) is not that of Cheshire. The pub was originally Mortlake House, built about 1777 by a banker, John

Cheshire Cheese, Nantwich.   *The Cheshire Tavern, Congleton.*

Johnson, and was one of the first houses to be built in the town during the prosperity generated from the silk industry. In 1945 it became a house used by older children for The National Children's Home. The exterior of the pub still keeps its dignified exterior.

CHESHIRE VIEW, Mow Cop. The pub is situated on a very steep road leading to the summit of the hill on which stands Mow Cop Castle, a folly built by Randle Wilbraham in 1754 to enhance the view from his country house, Rode Hall. The sign shows a view of the folly. Mow Cop is the birthplace of Primitive Methodism, which began when William Clowes held camp meetings here in 1807. There are splendid views from the inn across the Cheshire Plain.

CHESHIRE YEOMAN, Ledsham. The name may derive from a corruption of young man. A yeoman was a tenant or a farmer who cultivated his own freehold and as such had a reputation for being a freeman, not a servant and not one of the gentry, although he could work his way up to that position. The name was given to yeomanry regiments which were volunteer armies raised to protect the country from dangers such as the Armada (1558) or during the Napoleonic Wars. Yeomanry regiments were an essential part of the British Army especially in the First World War.

THE CHESTER BELL, Chester. The sign shows a jockey and horse riding past the winning post. The name refers to the winning bell on the nearby racecourse.

CHETWODE ARMS, Lower Whitley. This old pub dates from 1792 and the sign shows the arms of Lord Chetwode. These are quarterly argent and gules, four crosses pattée counter changed. Crest: out of a ducal coronet a lion rampant gules. The supporters are a crusader in chain mail and an officer of the 19th Royal Hussars. The motto is *corona mea Christus* (Christ my crown). Philip Chetwode from Buckinghamshire obtained lands in Nether Whitley in the seventeenth century on his marriage to Hester, heiress of William Touchet. The curious custom of roping takes place at the nearby St Luke's church. When a married couple leave the church, villagers hold them back by placing a rope across the path. On payment of a fee for a drink the rope is dropped and the couple can proceed on their way.

CHILDE OF HALE, Hale. John Middleton (1578-1623) was taken to London in order that he should fight the King's Wrestler. He won the bout, to the displeasure of James I who gave him £20 and told him to go back to Cheshire. Middleton was said to have grown to a height of 9ft 3ins (2.8m). His grave is in the churchyard within a railed enclosure and a statue stands nearby. The sign is based on a drawing now in Brasenose College, Oxford,

CHOLMONDELEY ARMS, Frodsham. This pub was built in 1891 according to the date on the gable. It was originally a beer-house known as the Albert Inn. The arms on the pub sign are sable, in chief two helmets in profile and in base a garb or. The coat of arms of the Cholmondeley family, however, has a red (gules) shield. The Cholmondeley family has been associated with Cheshire since the reign of Edward II (1284-1327) when Richard de Cholmondeley succeeded to his mother's manor of Cholmondeley in central Cheshire. The **Cholmondeley Arms**, Cholmondeley, was originally the village school, which closed in 1982. It was developed into an inn by the Marquis of Cholmondeley, which pacified the clientele as a former Marquis had closed all other public houses on land belonging to him.

CHURCH HOUSE, various locations. These pubs are usually situated near to a church, as is the **Church House** at Buglawton, noted for its magnificent flower displays, where the sign depicts the church of St John's, Buglawton. The **Church House** at Bollington, which also has a sign depicting the nearby church, contains numbered pew seats taken from the church. The **Church Green Hotel** at Lymm is the former vicarage.

CITY ARMS, Chester. (*See* **Temple Bar**.)

COACH & FOUR, Wilmslow. The sign shows a coach pulled by four horses.

COACH & HORSES, various locations. Most of the signs, as expected, display a coach laden with happy smiling passengers. The reality was very different as passengers battled with storms, rain and snow and often staggered off the coach half paralysed with the cold. One passenger wrote, 'Give me a collision, a broken axle and an

Cholmondeley Arms, Frodsham.

overturn, a runaway team, a drunken coachman, snowstorms, howling tempests, but heaven preserve me from floods'. Many coachmen had permanently bent fingers from constantly gripping the reins. Inns were vital for they provided refreshment to travellers and were stopping places where passengers could wait for the arrival of the coach. They also provided a change of horses so that many inns had large stables, which have now been converted to other uses. The coaching era also provided Britain with a universal timing mechanism. Until then, many areas had their own local time, but timekeeping for a coach was of the utmost necessity and it was now essential for a constant time to be recorded. The timing of the journey was therefore geared to the time set in London so that arrivals and departures had to be precisely observed. The **Coach & Horses**, Timbersbrook, near Congleton, displays a coachman urging on two horses pulling a coach in which can be seen a lady dressed in red. The coachman raises his whip to urge on the horses. The **Coach & Horses**, Neston, presents a sign of a coach drawn by four galloping horses with three passengers and the coachman on the roof of the coach.

THE COACHMAN, Hartford. This originally had a fine sign of the upper half of a coachman carrying a whip. The present sign shows a coachman driving a coach with four horses. On the roof are four top-hatted gentlemen. Another raises his hat. A lady holding a parasol sits behind the coachman. There may be some speculation as to how long she will hold the parasol once the coach starts to gallop and the winds starts to rise. The inn was originally the Station Hotel, which opened in 1837 when the line from London to Glasgow necessitated a station here. The station was frequently

The Coachman, Hartford.

used by Edward VII, then Prince of Wales, to stay with the Earl of Enniskillen for the hunting season.

THE COCK, various locations. This theme, which has been known since as early as the fourteenth century and may have indicated a venue for cockfighting (banned in 1835), has inspired many splendid signs such as **The Cock** at Henbury puffing out its chest as it crows to greet the rising sun. The **Cock Inn,** Northwich, has closed but the sign of a proud cock depicted in mosaic remains on the building.

COCK & PHEASANT, Bollington. The pub dates from 1755 and was originally three cottages, which were later incorporated into a pub. It may originally have been called The Cock. A black metal cut-out sign of a pheasant with a cock standing on the frame replaced the painted sign.

COCK O' BARTON, Barton. This pub, 600 years old, was once an old coaching inn and posting house. It once claimed to stock 200 different varieties of malt whisky, but these have been reduced to 68. Its name may have been derived from the fact that it allowed cockfighting. There have been extensive renovations but it still retains small rooms, which were the former coachmen's lodgings. The sign depicts a very proud cock holding a cup of tea or coffee.

Cock & Pheasant, Bollington.

COCK O' BUDWORTH, Great Budworth. This pub, reputedly built in the seventeenth century, has a sign showing a proud cock greeting the dawn. In the following century, it was a stopping place for 'Drunken' Barnaby who 'rolled around' the north of England visiting hostelries. Of the **Cock** he said:

> Thence to the' Cock at Budworth, where I
> Drank strong ale as brown as a berry:
> Till at last with deep health felled,
> To my bed I was compelled:
> I for state was bravely sorted,
> By two porters well supported.

COCK O'WITTON, Northwich. The earliest reference to this inn is 1742. The present building dates from 1932 but preserves the building line of the original. Its previous name was the Gamecock Inn.

COMBERMERE ARMS, Burleydam. There is a fine sign showing the arms of Viscount Combermere; quarterly first and four azure a chevron between three hanks of cotton, in chief a representation of the medal presented to the Viscount after the Battle of Salamanca (for Cotton); second and third quarterly argent a lion rampart sable (for Stapleton). The 1st supporters are two falcons with wings outstretched and supporting a spear from which flows a standard. The motto is *in utraque fortuna paratus* (prepared against all outcomes). The pub is reputed to have been haunted by a monk from Combermere Abbey. Two clergymen, however, persuaded the apparition to enter a bottle, which was placed under the entrance step. Combermere Abbey was a Cistercian house founded by Hugh Malbank in 1133. Although the monks were dedicated to poverty, they grew wealthy on the tolls extracted from the exploitation of Cheshire salt, and, as a result of this money, the abbey was greatly extended. It was dissolved at the Reformation in 1539 and the buildings and land were granted to Sir George Cotton, Vice Chancellor to Prince Edward, son and heir of Henry VIII. He demolished most of the buildings and built the present Combermere Hall, which incorporates much of the Abbot's House. Sir George's descendent, Sir Stapleton Cotton, was created Viscount Combermere. (*See* **Bhurtpore Inn** and **Lord Combermere**.)

COPPER MINE, Broxton. There is no sign but the pub is a reminder of a once important local industry. It contains memorabilia of that era.

COTTON ARMS, Wrenbury. This is the oldest pub in Wrenbury. The sign shows the arms of the Cotton family. The centre of the pub dates from the sixteenth century with parts of it said to have been built from ship's timbers. A tributary of the River Weaver flowed through the cellars until the early nineteenth century. Before the extension was built, it was said that the bar could only accommodate five people; the pub then had stabling for five horses.

CREWE ARMS, Crewe. This hotel, which was originally an inn, almost opposite the station, which was once the most important junction in the north midlands, is dominated by the sign of the heraldic arms of the Earl of Crewe, placed there when the hotel was finished in 1880. The Earldom of Crewe was elevated to a Marquisate in 1911 but the last marquis died in 1945 and the title became extinct. The family was descended from John Offley who married the daughter and heiress of John Crewe of Crewe Hall, and assumed her family name and arms incorporating them with his own. The arms are quarterly 1st and 4th azure, a lion rampant argent (for Crewe), 2nd and 3rd argent, a cross flory charged with a lion passant gold (for Offley). The supporters are a lion and a griffin and the crest is a lion's garb. The motto is *sequor non inferior* (I follow, not inferior). The colours are not produced exactly on the hotel sign. The interior of the hotel still has the appearance of a grand railway hotel with impressive marble fireplaces. The hotel included stables and organised horses and carriages, which could be hired by travellers to continue their journey.

CRICKETERS ARMS, Sandbach. The sign depicts a bowler at the end of his run when he has exerted his total effort in bowling the ball. This is unusual as most inn signs display a batsman. The sign of **The Cricketers Arms**, Widnes, shows two crossed cricket bats before a wicket and two cricket balls on the ground. The pub is known as 'The Leggies', not because this had anything to do with cricket, but because the first landlord had no legs.

CROSS KEYS, various locations. This symbol was often used in religious heraldry as being a reference to Christ's comment to St Peter: 'I will give unto you the keys of the kingdom of heaven' (Matthew 16:19). It was, however, deemed to be innocuous and so continued in use after the religious Reformation of the sixteenth century. The **Cross Keys**, Coppenhall, a former farmhouse, has two sets of crossed keys on its front gables. The **Cross Keys**, Chester, shows two keys, one gold, and one silver. Behind them is a somewhat sinister figure of a knight dressed in blue in a thoughtful pose with one hand over his mouth. **The Cross Keys**, Knutsford, a former eighteenth-century coaching inn, with its sign of two crossed keys, was mainly rebuilt in 1909.

CROWN, various locations. This was a popular name for a pub probably because it indicated loyalty to the monarch. The name was abolished during the Commonwealth (1649-1660) but reappeared in profusion once Charles II had been restored to the throne. The pub signs display a crown in some form, as does that of the **Crown Inn**, Goostrey. The **Crown Hotel**, Nantwich, originally the Crown and Sceptre, was rebuilt in 1585 on the site of an earlier inn destroyed in the Great Fire of 1583. Its sign depicts an ironwork sign of an imperial crown. The inn's third storey has a continuous gallery window with oak mullions, transoms and casements giving light to the Assembly Room. Part of the original wattle and daub construction can be seen in the foyer. During the Civil War it was used as a church because St Mary's church was used as a prison. It was an important coaching inn on the Chester to London route. The **Crown Inn**, Lower Peover, which was once a farmhouse, hosts the annual

Cricketers Arms, Sandbach.

gooseberry show, where prizes are given for the largest gooseberry grown in the area. The **Crown**, Northwich, has a record of licensees dating from 1778. It was known in 1775 as the Red Lion when Charles Machin bought it and changed the name to the **Crown**. It suffered from subsidence and was partly rebuilt in 1924. In the 1860s it was used for petty sessions and for the County Court. It was renamed the Swinging Witch for a few years from 1978 but recently has reverted to the name of the **Old Crown**. The sign of the **Crown**, Malpas, shows only half of an imperial crown. **The Crown**, Lymm, has a sign showing a King with a crown such as that worn by the early Plantagenet monarchs.

CUERDLY CROSS is the most westerly pub in Cheshire and is almost in the shadow of the eight cooling towers of the Fiddler's Ferry power station. The sign shows a Mr Pickwick character leaning against a small stone cross. At one side there is a red and white chequered cloth on the ground with a barm cake on it and a tankard overflowing with beer.

D

DANDY COCK, Disley. This is the name given to a bantam fowl, which is a vigorous fighter.

DAVENPORT ARMS, Calverley and **The Davenport** (originally The Davenport Arms) Marton, commemorate one of the oldest families in Cheshire, who once held the post of Master Sergeant and Chief Forester for most of the forested areas of Cheshire. They upheld forest laws with the utmost severity. Capesthorne Hall, seat of the Bromley Davenports contains a list of master robbers who were beheaded for breaking the laws. The Davenport crest, which is displayed with their arms on the sign at Marton, part of the Davenport estate, depicts a felon's head with a halter of gold round his neck. The arms are argent, a chevron between three crosslet fitchée sable. The Davenports added the name Bromley when they succeeded to the Bromley estates in 1822 and took over the seat at Capesthorne Hall. The present William Bromley Davenport is Lord Lieutenant of Cheshire. The Marton inn was part of the Davenport estate and acted as a courthouse where estate workers paid their rent.

DE TRAFFORD ARMS, Alderley Edge. The sign shows the arms of the De Trafford family: argent, a griffin gules. The crest is a thresher with a flail. There are two mottos: *now thus* and *gripe griffin hold fast*. The inn was first recorded in 1602 when it was a farmhouse occupied by the Trafford family. It stood by the side of a tollgate. In the 1870s it had an archery club, which was very popular with visitors from Manchester.

The Davenport, Marton.

DEE MILLER, Newton. There were several mills on the River Dee and there was constant friction between millers and townspeople about payments for grinding corn. The millers often asserted their independence and put a bold face on the dislike felt for them as well indicated by Isaac Bickerstaff in *The Song of the Miller of Dee* (1762): 'I care for nobody, no not I, and nobody cares for me.'

THE DOG INN, Over Peover. The sign shows a somewhat fed-up dog resting on its paws with what may be a bag of ice on the head. The expression may have something to do with the fact that this pub was called the Gay Dog until it was renamed in more politically correct times. The pub was created from a row of cottages built in 1804. It had been a grocer's, and a shoemaker's shop and then became a farm. It did not become a beer-house until 1806.

DOG & PARTRIDGE, Bollington. The sign shows the head of a black labrador holding a partridge in his mouth. Labradors are excellent retrievers. Pubs with these signs may once have been used to show that game birds were served there or that it was a venue for shooting parties.

THE DOLPHIN, Macclesfield. This name is usually associated with the sea and also appears as a heraldic crest. The sign shows a dolphin leaping out of the water. It is not clear why this pub has this name, when it is so far removed from the sea.

DROVERS ARMS, Allostock. A previous sign showed drovers driving their cattle. This pub was a stopping place for cattle drovers who drove cattle from the Welsh/Shropshire border to Manchester. In the nineteenth century drovers paid ½d a cow to pasture them in the field behind the pub.

DRUM & MONKEY, Alderley Edge and Comberbach. This was a popular sign from the seventeenth century and commemorates a familiar entertainment. Both signs show similar signs of a travelling showman, dressed in seventeenth-century costume, standing in a street, and turning an organ on which a monkey sits. The monkey usually beat on a drum to draw the attention of a crowd while the showman performed tricks. A second sign at the Alderley Edge inn has a close-up of the man and his monkey.

DUBLIN PACKET, Chester. Chester was once an important port before the River Dee silted up and the trade transferred to the River Mersey. A packet boat travelled regularly between Chester and Dublin. The pub contains photographs of old Cheshire and mementoes of the footballer Dixie Dee who was the landlord here for many years.

DUKE OF BRIDGEWATER, Crewe has a sign purporting to be a portrait of the duke. (*See* **Bridgewater Arms**.)

DUKE OF GLOUCESTER, Crewe. This is a new pub. The sign has on one side a portrait of a young Prince Henry, Duke of Gloucester (1900-74), son of George V and brother of King George VI, and on the other a railway engine named Duke of Gloucester. This engine was the Pacific Class No.7100 built at Crewe in the 1940s and intended to be the forerunner of a new generation of heavy express locomotives. This never materialised as first diesel and later electric engines replaced steam.

DUKE OF PORTLAND, Lach Dennis. The pub was originally called The Portland Arms. The sign shows the head and shoulders of an upper-class gentleman, smoking a large cigar. This may refer to an eighteenth-century Duke of Portland, one of the many Army commanders who set up their soldiers as pub landlords when the Army had no more use for their services. The name was also one of several pseudonyms used by Edward VII, when Prince of Wales. He often visited Cheshire to accompany the Cheshire Hunt.

DUN COW, Ollerton. Dun is Old English for brown. The pub was originally the courthouse of Bucklow Hundred. The snug was the magistrates' room.

THE DURHAM HEIFER, Broxton. This pub, once a farmhouse, has a cartoon sign depicting the startled face of a heifer with a very long neck; round the neck hangs a cow bell. A Durham or Craven heifer is one that has not had a calf. The most famous one, mentioned at Gargrave-in-Craven in 1807, weighed over a ton and was depicted on banknotes issued in 1817 by the Yorkshire Bank.

The Dog Inn, Over Peover.

The Dolphin, Macclesfield.

Drum & Monkey, Alderley Edge.

Duke of Gloucester, Crewe.

Duke of Portland, Lach Dennis.

The Durham Heifer, Broxton.

DURHAM OX, Congleton and Macclesfield. An ox, bred by Charles Collings of Ketton, near Darlington, in 1796 weighed over two tons by the time it was six years old. To make the most of this splendid animal, its owner proudly showed it during a tour throughout the country, hence the animal, being so well known, was later displayed on pub signs. Collings sold the animal in 1801 at 216 stone. It was then sold twice and the second buyer kept it until 1812. When it was slaughtered, it weighed over 180 stone. The Congleton sign shows the animal, whose size does not seem to portray its reputation, lowering its head at a surprised dairymaid. The Macclesfield bull is a more respectable size.

THE DUSTY MILLER, Wrenbury. This is an appropriate name for an inn situated most picturesquely opposite Wrenbury Mill, by the side of the Shropshire Union Canal. It was originally a working mill until the twentieth century when it became a gathering place for local produce and storing cheeses. It was derelict in 1971 but renovation in 1977 created this attractive inn. Thomas Telford designed the bridge across the canal.

DYSART ARMS, Bunbury. The pub with its cosy interior lined with paintings and etchings, has an extension, which includes a wall of library books. The pub displays the arms of the Earl of Dysart, which were also the arms of the Tollemache family: argent a fret sable. The crest should be a winged horse's head argent, but the horse's head on the sign is striped in red and white. The supporters are two stags. Dating back to the eighteenth century, it was originally a farmhouse owned by a branch of the Tollemache family, which in the next century began selling ales and thus becoming the village pub. The Earls of Dysart, a Scottish peerage, were settled in Fife. The peerage can pass into the female line and did do on the death of the 9th earl in 1935. The association of the name with Cheshire began in 1680 when the 3rd Earl of Dysart, who resided at Ham House in Surrey, married Grace Wilbraham, daughter of Sir Thomas Wilbraham, 3rd baronet of Woodley, and his sole heiress. On the death of Sir Thomas, Grace succeeded to 20,000 acres of Cheshire including Beeston Castle and the Woodley Estate. Later this became the Peckforton Estate. A maternal grandson of the 4th earl, John Jervis Tollemache, MP for Chester (1841-68) and West Cheshire (1868-72), was created Baron Tollemache in 1876. He commissioned Anthony Salvin to build Peckforton Castle.

E

THE EARL, Crewe. This was formerly the Earl of Crewe and once had a sign with a portrait of the last earl and a painting of Crewe Hall. (*See* **Crewe Arms**.) On the gable there is a terracotta panel showing the head of Queen Victoria and images of her empire to commemorate her diamond jubilee, which indicates that the pub was built in 1887.

EARL OF CHESTERS, Crewe. This pub was originally the Earl of Chesters Own and once had a sign showing a portrait of a soldier in uniform. The Earl of Chester's Own Yeomanry was one of the last regiments to fight on horses. Yeomanry regiments were raised about 1804 to fight the threat of a Napoleonic invasion and retained their independence from the regular Army. Thus they could not be sent overseas, until 1914, unless they volunteered to go. Their training was often spasmodic and possibly more ceremonial than practical. They expressed their independence in the ornate uniforms they wore, often designed by the man who had raised them. They proved their worth, however, when they fought, often in very bloody battles, during the First World War. The name of this pub is worth a comment as one title of the Prince of Wales is the Earl of Chester and the yeomanry regiment had the Prince of Wales feathers as its cap badge.

EAGLE AND CHILD. Both pubs bearing this name have now closed, that at Nether Alderley is now a house and the one in Northwich is a bank. The name, however, is worth a comment. It is linked to the Stanley family, who were Lords of Man but given land in Cheshire by Richard III before he was betrayed by Lord Stanley, who switched sides at the Battle of Bosworth Field in 1485. The Eagle and Child, which may still be seen carved above the HSBC Bank in Northwich, was the crest of the Stanley family. Legend has it that Sir Thomas Latham had a son by Mary Oscatel, a serving woman with whom he was having an illicit affair. He wanted this son to inherit his estates and so told his servant to put his son at the foot of a tree frequented by an eagle. He calculated that if he took his wife on a walk past the tree, she would hear the child's cries and be so moved that she would adopt the baby. This she did and, on the request of Sir Thomas, the child was called Oscatel Latham. Not all turned out as Sir Thomas had wished. On his deathbed he confessed what he had done. The boy was disinherited and Thomas's daughter inherited the estate. She later married Sir John Stanley and the lands passed to that family. Sir Thomas had adopted the eagle as his crest but the Stanley family preferred to have a crest of an eagle looking rapaciously down on a child. (*See* **Stanley Arms**.)

EGERTON ARMS, various locations. The name is not an unexpected one as the Egerton family, with its several branches, were, and still are, landowners in Cheshire. Their arms are depicted on a number of pubs, including that of the **Egerton Arms** at Astbury, which dates back to the eighteenth century, when the family held the manors of Newbold and Astbury. The pub is reputed to have a resident ghost. In 1906 Edward Spendlow, who lived in the house next door to the pub, attacked his sister-in-law Margaret Slater. She later died as a result and Spendlow was hanged at Chester for this crime. Why Margaret should haunt the pub, however, is unclear. As well as the sign at Astbury, the **Egerton Arms**, Saughall and the **Egerton Arms**, Chester, also display the arms: argent, a lion rampant gules between three pheons (arrowheads) sable. The crest is a lion rampant holding an arrow pointing downwards. The supporters are a lion and a wyvern. The motto is *sic donec* (thus until). The **Egerton Arms**, Broxton, has a sign depicting the Grey-Egerton coat of arms with the arms of Grey quartered with the arms of Egerton and two crests one for Grey and one for Egerton. The motto is *virtuti non armis fido* (I trust in courage not arms). The Grey-Egertons have held land in the local area since the thirteenth century.

THE ELEPHANT, Shavington. The sign depicts an elephant joyously raising its left leg as it happily galumphs along. On its back is its owner, crouched in a howdah, and its mahout controller. The pub, which has been a brew house and a shop, was originally called the Elephant and Castle. There are two explanations as to the origins of this inn sign. The first is that the name may refer to the crest of the Worshipful Company of Cutlers, whose grant of arms dates from 1476, which has elephant with a howdah on its back. The link was probably because cutlery has ivory handles, which were obtained from elephants' tusks. The second is that it is a corruption of the name of the *Infanta de Castile*, referring to Eleanor of Castile, the respected and admired wife of Edward I, King of England (1272-1307).

ENGINE HOUSE TAVERN, Broughton. This inn is so called because engineers used to pump water from the pumping station across the road by the river.

The Elephant, Shavington.

F

THE FALCON, Chester, originally **The Golden Falcon**. The sign shows a falcon descending to seize its prey in its claws. The building is a seventeenth-century one, but it stands above a thirteenth-century crypt. It was renovated in 1886 and was completely restored in 1982. There is a continuous band of windows on the first floor that lights the upstairs lounge. Handel stayed here before he sailed to Dublin to conduct the first official performance of *Messiah*. As he was delayed in sailing he tried out his composition in the cathedral engaging the best singers in the city. One man, Joinson, took the bass part. A rehearsal took place at this inn. Joinson failed to sing the right notes. Handel lost his temper: 'You schantrel, 'tit not you dell me dat you could sing on soite'. 'Yes, sir, said Joinson, 'so I can, but not at first sight.'

FARMERS ARMS, various locations. The sign, like that on the **Farmers Arms**, Congleton, is often depicted as a punning one. On the shield are three ears of corn. The crest above the helmet is a red bull with white spots and the supporters are shirt-sleeved, farm labourers armed with sickles. This is set on a blue background. Changes to signs occur very suddenly. The previous sign had a green background. There was no helmet and a white bull was placed on a white shield, a chief in blue, three wheatears and two farm workers as supporters. The **Farmers Arms** at Delamere was originally a bakehouse. The **Farmers Arms** at Huxley is reputed to date from the seventeenth century. It was once a butcher's shop and claims to have been a hospital for wounded men during the Civil War. The **Farmers Arms**, Wilmslow, depicts a somewhat funereal scene in black of a farmer ploughing his land with two shire horses. The **Farmers Arms**, Lymm, shows two farmers possibly discussing their crops, one with a staff in his hand.

THE FERRY TAVERN, Fiddler's Ferry, Penketh, is by the Sankey Canal, which is navigable to here but all boats except canoes and rowing boats are stopped by the concrete bridge. There are spectacular views across the Mersey. The name dates back to 1160 when the manor of Penketh was in the hands of a man called Fidler. The right to have a ferry was one of his perquisites. The building, with its stone flagged floors, originally the ferryman's house, became an inn in 1760.

FIDDLE I'TH BAG, Burtonwood. There were originally two pictures on different signs. One showed a wandering fiddler; such a man always carried his fiddle around in a bag. The other showed a seventeenth-century sowing device, a seed fiddle. The present sign shows a fiddle and the bag in which it is kept.

FLOWERPOT, various locations. Macclesfield has two pubs of this name. One at Hurdsfield, which has a sign of a pot planted with flowers, was converted into a pub from one house in a row of cottages in 1927; the other is a new pub which has changed its sign several times. The present sign of this pub shows a large plant pot from which spring red and white flowers. In the background is a gardener by his potting shed against which his tools rest. This sign of the Flowerpot once had a religious origin depicting the Angel Gabriel visiting the Virgin Mary (*See* **Angel**), the two often being separated by a lily in a flowerpot. After the Reformation the sign fell out of favour and depicted only the angel or a flowerpot. It is not suggested, however, that either of the Macclesfield inns had any religious connection.

FISHPOOL, Delamere, This is suitably named as it close by a pool. The sign shows a trout leaping out of the water.

THE FOOL'S NOOK, Sutton. A former sign showed a jester as this area was said to be the meeting place of court jesters but it more likely that the area got its name from the old Cheshire word 'nook', which meant a bend as the pub is situated where the road takes a decisive bend here. The new owners, however, have changed the sign to one showing a barge sailing on the nearby Macclesfield Canal which they think is more in keeping with the district name of Oakwood.

Above: *The Fool's Nook, Sutton.*

Left: *Fiddle I'th Bag, Burtonwood.*

Foresters Arms, Winterley.

FORESTERS ARMS, various locations. The Ancient Order of Foresters was one of the many Friendly Societies founded in the nineteenth century to help men in trade. The Foresters claimed to be the oldest of these societies, enrolling Adam and Eve as its first members! A weekly subscription paid for help in case of injury, sickness, and infirmity in old age and to pay burial expenses, which was essential so that members would not be buried in a pauper's grave. Most of these societies had their headquarters in pubs. It is not suggested, however, that all pubs bearing these names were linked to these societies. The **Foresters Arms** at Delamere is dated to 1880. Many of the signs are punning signs. The **Foresters Arms** Tarporley depicts a white shield with a hunting horn on it. Above is a crest of a hand holding an axe. The **Foresters Arms**, Winterley, has a punning heraldic sign with four quarters: two hands clasped in friendship, two stags running, a horn placed below a chevron and a horn and quiver. The original sign of the **Foresters Arms**, Congleton, showed a forester, sitting on a fallen tree, holding a foaming tankard in his left hand. By his foot was a pudding basin wrapped in a white cloth. This was a man obviously enjoying his rest. The present sign shows the upper part of a woodman holding an axe firmly across his body. (*See* **Oddfellows Arms**.)

THE FOX, Haslington. A fox has been a very popular sign since at least the fifteenth century and is an appropriate one for the country area of Cheshire. The pub has been rebuilt several times but the present sign is a dramatic one showing a fox sitting in the

The Fox Inn, Sandbach.

snow by a stark black branch. The sign of **The Fox Inn**, Sandbach, shows an alert fox warily peering from the bushes.

FOX AND BARREL, Cotebrook, Little Budworth. This was originally the Kings Head but received its present name because a landlord gave shelter to a fox in his cellar when hounds were pursuing it, and set it free when the hunt had gone.

FOX AND HOUNDS, Tilston. This former coaching inn has now closed but it still retains its amusing sign of a fox resting on the branch of a tree while bewildered hounds mill round beneath it.

THE FRANKLIN, Macclesfield. The sign shows a bearded man with a rifle over his shoulder standing in an icy waste. In the background is a ship. Sir John Franklin (1786-1847) was an English naval officer who led two expeditions to the Canadian Arctic. In 1843 he set out again to search for the North West Passage but the expedition was lost. A search party found evidence that the expedition had become icebound. The Canadian arctic administration district of Franklin is named after him.

FREEMASONS ARMS, various locations. Freemasons in their original guise were itinerant stonemasons who travelled from place to place in the medieval period seeking work. The present freemasons often use pubs as their meeting places and

The Franklin, Macclesfield.   *Freemasons, Northwich.*

The Frozen Mop, Great Warford.

the name may have lingered. Many pub signs are part of the punning tradition. The **Freemasons**, Northwich, has a well at the rear made from stones believed to come from the Roman fort in the area. The sign shows a chevron on which are compasses, between three castles. Above the shield is a helm surmounted by a castle surrounded by ornate mantling.

THE FRIAR PENKETH, Warrington. The pub is on the site of a thirteenth-century Augustinian friary. One of the scholars was Friar Penketh (d. 1482). The sign depicts a friar sitting at a desk, head resting on his arm, placed against a stylised church constructed of black and white squares.

THE FROZEN MOP, Great Warford, Mobberley. This was originally the Warford Arms until 1950. There are several versions of the present name. The most reliable says that the landlady kept a mop and bucket outside to clear away the filth but these were frozen solid by a sudden frost. The sign shows a somewhat startled woman gazing at a frozen mop, which she has taken out of a bucket. The pub was completely renovated in 2007.

FROG, Upton. The name comes from Frog Hall, now demolished, which once stood by the side of the pub.

G

GEORGE & DRAGON, various locations. St George is the patron saint of England who ironically has no distinctive connection with this country. There are two suggestions as to his origin. George of Cappadocia was described by the historian Edward Gibbon as 'an energetic and unscrupulous pork contractor', yet he became the Bishop of Alexandria (AD 356-61). But churches had already been dedicated to him in the Near East some fifty years earlier. The original St George therefore seems to have been a soldier from Lydda in Palestine, who was martyred during the reign of the Emperor Diocletian about AD 303. His cult came into England when Richard I (1189-99), who had had a vision assuring him of the saint's protection, encouraged the knights who accompanied him on the Third Crusade to wear a surcoat of a red cross on a white background and to dedicate themselves to St George. Edward III (1327-77) named him as England's patron saint and in 1344 founded the order of the Garter with St George and the dragon on its badge. St George's name became a rousing battle cry as recalled by Shakespeare: 'Cry God for Harry! England and St George!' (*Henry V*, act 3, sc. 1, l. 31). The dragon was added as a symbol of the fight between good and evil but *The Golden Legend* says that St George saved the life of a princess who was about to be sacrificed in order to propitiate a dragon, which had terrorised the country. St George defeated the dragon whereupon many people hastened to be baptised and reject their cruel ways. The legend therefore represents the triumph of good over evil and as such the Church promulgated it. His feast day is 23 April. The **George & Dragon**, Great Budworth, has a splendid iron sign of St George spearing the dragon whose tail is twisted around one leg of the horse. At the entrance to the car park is a mounting block used by women or elderly gentlemen to help them mount their horses. The inn is a remodelled Arts and Crafts style building rebuilt by Piers Edgerton Warburton of Arley and the architect, John Douglas of Sandiway. The aim was to provide much better accommodation for good behaviour when drinking. To emphasise the theme of sobriety, other pubs in the village were closed down and the following inscription was placed above the door:

> As St George in armed array did the fiery dragon slay,
> So might thou with might no less slay the dragon drunkenness.

The **George & Dragon**, Holmes Chapel, was known as the George as early as 1752 when Charles Vernon kept it. He then altered the name to the New Red Lion to compete with the Red Lion pub and hired out post chaises and horses. Later the pub took on its present name. It was demolished in 1970 for road widening and rebuilt. The sign is a crusading St George, riding his horse, rising above the dragon to smite it with his sword. The **George & Dragon**, Hurdsfield, began life as a school for young ladies. The **George and Dragon**, Tarvin, once had a mural showing life in the village but this was destroyed in a fire a few years ago. The sign is an unusual one of St George fighting off a rearing dragon, which is about to plunge its massive claws into the horse's chest. The sign of the **George & Dragon**, Winsford, shows a most saintly saint with a halo round his head, riding over a green dragon. There are cartoons and sketches of royalty inside. The **George & Dragon**, Macclesfield, has a sign of St George rearing up to spear a scaly dragon who desperately shoots out its red tongue at the saint.

GLOBE, various locations. A globe usually indicates the universality of the world or that the former British Empire extended across the world. It may also have indicated that port was sold in the pub. The **Globe**, Mow Cop dates from the nineteenth century. **The Globe**, Stapeley is reputed to be haunted. It has a splendid sign of two men dressed in sixteenth-century costume pointing to a globe. One is in purple with blue hose and white ruff. The other, obviously the traveller or explorer, is dressed in brown, with a green cloak and hat with a black plume. Seemingly, he is intending to expand his horizons.

GOLDEN EAGLE, Chester. This pub has a sign of an eagle swooping on its prey. It claims to have the unusual sight of the ghosts of Roman legionaries marching through the walls of the cellar, which would then correspond to the Roman ground level.

GOLDEN FLEECE, Lymm. This building, by the side of the Shropshire Union Canal, dates from the sixteenth century. In Greek mythology, Jason and the Argonauts sought

George and Dragon, Tarvin.

George & Dragon, Great Budworth.

The Globe, Stapeley.

Golden Eagle, Chester.

the Golden Fleece. The Order of the Golden Fleece, founded in 1430 by Philip, Duke of Burgundy, and sometimes bestowed upon Englishmen, had a ram with a red band round its middle as its badge.

GOLDEN LION, various locations. This is a heraldic badge of Henry I, of the Percy family, Dukes of Northumberland and of several London guilds. It was also a badge of Flemish traders who introduced hops into England so that ale could be produced as beer. The **Golden Lion**, Frodsham, was originally called the White Horse between 1812-35, but the cellars were is use well before that date. There is an excellent sign of a rampant golden lion on a blue shield. The crest is a lion's head, which is surrounded by mantling. The **Golden Lion**, Middlewich, has two signs: one depicts the traditional lion rampant; the other shows a resting lion staring across the African veldt.

THE GOLDEN PHEASANT, Plumley. Pheasants are a common sight in the Cheshire countryside and this 3-D sign shows a pheasant in all its glory. The pheasant theme recurs throughout the pub. (*See* also **Pheasant**.)

THE GOSHAWK, Mouldsworth. A goshawk is a large, almost buzzard-size bird with short wings. It is a popular bird with falconers who call the female bird a goshawk and the male bird a tercel. This pub, near to the station, was originally called the Station Hotel. It is now a pleasant meeting place for those who visit the nearby Motor Museum.

Golden Lion, Frodsham. Golden Lion, Middlewich.

GRAND JUNCTION, Crewe. Crewe owes its existence as a town to the Grand Junction Railway Co., when it chose the site for its railway engineering works in 1840. Its paternalistic concern for its workers ensured that it built houses, schools, churches, roads and pubs. It also provided a library and recreation facilities including Queens Park. The Grand Junction pub was first built in 1838 and rebuilt in 1844. This was demolished in the 1960s when the present town centre was laid out and a new pub rebuilt near to the original site. It is a pity that the engine on the sign is not one of the original Grand Junction ones.

GRAPES, various locations. This is a popular name for a pub as once indicating that it sold wine. **The Grapes** at Runcorn was previously a farmhouse and had its own brewery. The sign shows a woman, sitting in a vineyard, holding a bunch of grapes. A large bunch is placed in each of the lower corners.

GREEN DRAGON, Lymm. The green dragon was the badge of the Earls of Pembroke. Here a flying dragon is sketched in outline on the wall of the inn. The **Green Dragon**, Northwich, with its sign of a rearing green dragon, was originally built about 1810 with stables to provide transport for travellers. It was rebuilt in 1870 and is a good example of a Victorian public house although part of it was extended in the twentieth century. The **Green Dragon**, Heatley, has a cartoon sign showing the head of a green dragon breathing fire and contemplating the helmeted head of a somewhat dazed knight.

The Grey Horse, Glazebury.

GREENLAND FISHERY, Neston. This sixteenth-century pub gets its name from Liverpool fishermen who made it their headquarters when they went to hunt whales off Greenland.

GREY HORSE, various locations. A grey horse appears to be grey because of its black and white hairs. **The Grey Horse**, a former coaching inn at Glazebury was originally called the Grey Doctor.

GREYHOUND, Ashley. This was originally a farm and was first called the Orell Arms after Robert Orell of nearby Arden House. In 1841 it became part of the Tatton Estate and was renamed the Greyhound after Lord Egerton's favourite dog. The **Greyhound**, Saughall, was once a customs house at the busy port of Saughall, which dealt with Chester's trade. It was renovated in 1993 and again in 2000 to extend the building and is now a cosy pub, with log fires in winter, somewhat distant from the river. A greyhound was also the badge of Henry VII.

THE GRIFFIN, Widnes, has a sign showing this heraldic beast rampant in gold on a white shield.

GROSVENOR ARMS, Chester. Grosvenor is the family name of the Dukes of Westminster who own extensive lands in Cheshire and London. The Grosvenor family fortunes began when Sir Thomas Grosvenor married the heiress Mary Davis in

1677 thereby gaining land, which became some of the richest estate lands in London. The **Grosvenor Arms**, Pulford is an eighteenth-century coaching inn.

THE GROVE, various locations. Most signs display a tranquil grove of trees, as does that of The **Grove Inn**, Congleton. This inn may have been sited to indicate the most westward extension of the town wood mentioned in the Domesday Book (1086). A variation of the name, but with a similar sign of a woodland, is the **Woodland Grove**, Ellesmere Port.

H

HAMMER AND PINCERS, Widnes. The sign represents a forge with the instruments lying on the anvil. The building dates from the 1700s and is the second oldest pub in the town. Inside are oak beams and a stone fireplace. The booths have stained glass panels.

HANGING GATE, various locations. The **Hanging Gate**, Langley is partly an early seventeenth-century building with extensive views of the Pennines and over the Cheshire Plain. This was once a drovers' inn giving shelter on a remote location in the Cheshire Peak District. The locals knew it as Tom Steeles', nicknaming it after a one-armed landlord who kept the pub for over fifty years. It is an extremely popular place with walkers and there are panoramic views over the moors. One sign shows a medieval man, stick and bag over shoulder, tankard held high in the air obviously telling tall stories to a bemused couple. A second sign, which is also that of The **Hanging Gate**, Weaverham, has the usual inscription:

> This Gate hangs here
> And Troubles None.
> Refresh and Pay
> and Travel On.

The Weaverham pub has a water pump at the rear and a stone mounting block at the front.

HARE AND HOUNDS, Crowton. This 300-year-old pub has a suitable name, as it is one of the meeting places of the Cheshire Hunt. There are two signs. One shows a hare frantically running while two hounds loom over it. The other displays a hare calmly sitting on one side of a stream while two frustrated hounds are on the other bank.

HARP INN, Little Neston. The harp is associated with both Wales and Ireland. The harp was first adopted by Henry VIII as an Irish badge and James I incorporated it into the royal coat of arms. The name may have been adopted for this out of the way pub because Neston and Little Neston once had sailors coming to these villages from both those countries, when it was once a busy port. Now the river has silted up and grass grows alongside the quay, and there are views across the silted-up estuary to the Welsh coast. The isolated pub, converted from two cottages, has two small rooms. There are two signs: a metal harp and a painted sign showing a harp between a building with a large chimney and an industrial wharf. This refers to the time when coalminers used the pub and inside the building are photographs of the last shift. A nearby quay, built in the 1760s, was the site from which shiploads of coal were exported to Ireland. The coal was extracted from the nearby Wirral Colliery from about 1760 to 1928. In the vicinity are some small slagheaps.

HARRINGTON ARMS, various locations. The Earls of Harrington held lands in Sutton, Gawsworth and Bosley. The **Harrington Arms**, Gawsworth was a working farm for almost 500 years. The main part is a three-storey brick building dating from the late-seventeenth or early eighteenth century. It still contains some of the original furniture in two public rooms, which have quarry-tiled floors. The **Harrington Arms**, Bosley, has a sign showing the coat of arms of the Harrington family: quarterly ermine and gules, in the centre a crescent on a crescent for cadency. The crest is a tower azure from which issues the upper half of a rampant lion.

THE HARROW, Culcheth, is a modern pub but one of the few in Cheshire depicting a harrow. In this case it has been placed in a field after the farmer has used it.

THE HATTER, Warrington. The sign shows a hatter blocking out a bowler hat. This pub was originally called the Mad Hatter. Lewis Carroll immortalised the Mad Hatter in *Alice in Wonderland*, when the hatter joined the March Hare and the Dormouse at a tea party. Sir John Tenniel drew him in a top hat and a teacup in his hand. Hatters were said to be mad because the use of mercurial nitrate in the making of felt hats may have made them behave oddly. The phrase, however, may have been mad (angry) as an adder, rather than mad as a hatter. Warrington is so proud of the Mad Hatter that it has an eight-ton granite statue of the tea party in Golden Square.

HATTON ARMS, Hatton, is a seventeenth-century cottage now converted to an inn with two signs, one over the door and another in the car park. Both display the former arms of the county of Cheshire: azure, a chevron between three garbs. Until 1873 this inn was the Red Lion. Henry III gave the township to William, son of Hothy of Hatton.

Harp Inn, Little Neston.

The Harrow, Culcheth.

HAWK INN, Haslington. This is a very old building dating back to the sixteenth century with parts of it still containing the original wattle and daub. The hanging sign shows an alert hawk resting on a branch and there is also a stone sign of a hawk dropping, claws at the ready, towards its prey. The outside walls are decorated with curious heads and inscriptions in capital letters, such as, 'A jug of ale, a whispered word can be found within these old walls' and 'Duck or grouse all ye who enter here.'

HAZEL PEAR, Acton Bridge. This variety of pear was used for wine and cider. There is no sign but a tree grows in the garden of the pub, hence the name.

HEADLESS WOMAN, Duddon. Although pub signs with this name are often referring to women who are depicted without their heads because they talked too much, this pub is reputed to be named after a woman who worked at Hockenhull Hall. She was beheaded by Cromwell's troops either for not revealing the hiding places of villagers or because she refused to reveal where her mistress's jewellery was hidden. Her ghost is said to walk between the hall and the pub. The sign shows in outline a headless woman holding her head under her right arm. The previous sign was a ship's carving showing a headless woman. Unfortunately this was stolen.

HERMIT, Hermitage Green, Croft. This pub shows a hermit sitting in front of a fire apparently toasting some food.

HIGHWAYMAN, Rainow, dates from the late fifteenth century and is said to refer to a local highwayman who preyed on travellers making their way along what was then a lonely road and looking out for them from a nearby vantage point. Highwaymen were dreaded during the stagecoach era when they preyed on travellers going about their normal business. One of the most famous was Richard (Dick) Turpin (1706-39) who was hanged at York for his crimes. He is associated with several Cheshire pubs although it is not entirely certain that he harried the west of England.

THE HINDERTON ARMS, Neston. The pub is on the site of the old courthouse. The arms on the sign are those of the Earls of Shrewsbury. (*See* **Shrewsbury Arms**.)

HOLLY BUSH, various locations. The **Holly Bush**, Little Leigh, which probably dates from the fifteenth century, is the only pub in the country with no bar. It is still part pub, part farmhouse. The **Holly Bush**, Bollington was originally called the Shoulder of Mutton where beer was brewed in the late nineteenth century. The archway to the right of the pub was used as a slaughterhouse. During the 1880's depression in the textile industry, the landlord, Jesse Beard, brewed broth which he served to out of work mill-workers. The sign usually depicts the bush alone but this pub has a yellow-breasted bird resting in the bush. The **Holly Bush Inn**, Winterley, has a sign showing a large bush and at its side a single sprig of holly.

Hawk Inn, Haslington.

HOP POLE, Warrington. Hop bines used to be trained up poles and sometimes pubs put them outside their premises to advertise that they were selling beer. The sign for this pub is of a man wearing a red waistcoat drawing a tankard of beer from a barrel. Over this trails hops. Actors from a nearby theatre, which has now closed, once used the theatre bar.

THE HORNS, various locations. The name is usually associated with post horns used by stagecoach guards to announce their arrival or to warn a tollgate keeper to open the gate. The name of **The Horns** at Little Leigh is obvious from a pair of horns hung over the bar and the huge ox horns placed above the outside door. Above is the date 1734.

HORSESHOE, various locations. A horseshoe on a sign must be depicted upright otherwise the inn's luck will run out, and the sign of **The Horseshoe** at Croft is a correct one. The **Horse Shoe Inn**, Willaston (near Crewe), has a sign of a brewer's dray loaded with barrels, galloping within a horseshoe. This pub brewed beer from 1937 in a simple wooden hut at the back, very useful during the Second World War when it supplied pubs over a wide area thus relieving a shortage. The comedian Frankie Howerd stayed here when he was performing at the Lyceum Theatre, Crewe and often served behind the bar. The sign of the **Horseshoe** at Kingsley shows a blacksmith pulling nails out of a horseshoe while the horse patiently waits to be re-shod.

Headless Woman, Duddon.

Holly Bush Inn, Winterley.

HORSE AND JOCKEY, Helsby. Horse racing as a sport is said to date from the reign of Henry II (1154-89). Many sovereigns have supported it, hence its nickname, the sport of Kings. The Jockey Club, formed in 1750, regulates the sport. The most famous racecourse in Cheshire is the Roodee at Chester, but many villages once held point-to-points and local races.

I

IRON GREY, Sandbach. This is another name for a grey horse of a dead lead colour, and the sign depicts a horse with the appropriate colouring.

THE IVY HOUSE, Macclesfield. The name comes from the nearby Ivy Lane but the sign shows the gable end of a house entirely covered with ivy.

Iron Grey, Sandbach.

The Jolly Sailor, Macclesfield.

J

JOLLY SAILOR, Macclesfield. The sign shows the head of a sailor with the traditional headgear and neckerchief worn in the late-nineteenth and early twentieth century.

JOLLY THRESHER, Broomedge, Lymm. This eighteenth-century pub has a sign showing a man threshing in a barn with a flail. Behind him stretches a large cornfield.

K

KILTON INN, Mere. This pub was named after a racehorse. Dick Turpin is said to have used this house and to have drunk here after he had killed a person in Altrincham. Part of the pub was the local courtroom with cells in the cellar.

KING WILLIAM, Wilmslow. The sign represents the head of William IV (1785-1837), the third son of George III, who became King (1830-37). Probably on account of his royal connection, he became an Admiral of the Fleet in 1801 and was known as the

Sailor King. It is reasonably reported that he introduced the tradition in the navy of giving the royal toast sitting down because he kept banging his head against the low ceiling of the wardroom when rising for the royal toast.

KINGS ARMS, various locations. **The Kings Arms**, Middlewich, is one of the oldest pubs in the town and still has some of its original wattle and daub. It has the traditional sign of the royal coat of arms and supporters of a lion and a unicorn. Below is the motto, *Dieu et Mon Droit* (God and My Right). The lions of England were the heraldic animals of the Kings of England; the unicorn, the heraldic animal of the Kings of Scotland, was added when James VI of Scotland became James I of England in 1603. The **Kings Arms**, Crewe has a sign showing a medieval King wearing a surcoat bearing the royal arms, riding a horse and holding a drawn sword. **The Kings Arms**, Wilmslow, has the royal coat of arms on a shield with a cap of maintenance above it and surmounted by a lion.

KINGS HEAD, various locations. This is a very popular sign and usually displays a portrait of a monarch, Henry VIII being the most popular. **The Kings Head**, Chester, is a former coaching inn, built in the sixteenth century. The **Kings Head**, Warrington, has an unusual sign of a bearded and moustached medieval King, wearing a surcoat with the lions of England and the lilies of France. Round his pointed helmet is a gold circlet crown.

KING'S LOCK, Middlewich. This has no sign but the lock is name enough. The pub was an ale and porterhouse for bargees at the junction of the Trent and Mersey Canal and the Shropshire Union Canal and is still a popular stopping place for pleasure barges. It was built of stack construction. The lower part was for storage and the upper part had the bar. The brick bridge over the canal is the only entrance to the pub and must have been built by James Brindley when he was constructing the canal.

THE KNOT, Ellesmere Port. The sign displays this wading bird, which winters on the Dee estuary.

King's Lock, Middlewich.

L

LAMB, various locations. The lamb was originally a religious sign associated with Christ and a number of saints – St John the Baptist, St Agnes and St Catherine. It is also used as a heraldic sign by a number of guilds if they are connected with the woollen trade. **The Lamb**, Willaston, is now the headquarters of the local football club, which plays on a pitch at the rear.

LEATHER'S SMITHY, Macclesfield Forest. The pub overlooks Ridgegate Reservoir. It developed from a former smithy when William Leather, a local farrier in 1821 got a licence to sell ale and porter. The sign depicts him pounding on his anvil.

LEGH ARMS, Adlington. The Legh family has been established in Cheshire since the fourteenth century. In 1315, a female descendant of the last member of the De Corona family, who had been granted the manor of Adlington in the thirteenth century, married John de Legh. The family still resides at the nearby Adlington Hall. **Legh Arms**, Prestbury. This sixteenth-century building was added to during the seventeenth century. Ranulph Legh, son of Robert Legh of Adlington, provided money to build the tower of the parish church, and there is a monument to the Leghs in the church. Earlier the pub was known as the Blackamore's Head as in 1719 a painter put a black person's head on the sign. At one time the pub displayed the Legh Arms and a Black Boy but has now a sign depicting the quartered Legh Arms and the motto *da glorium Deo*. The words 'Black Boy' have been added below the sign.

LEGS OF MAN, Smallwood. The pub, although rebuilt in 1939, certainly is on the site of an earlier one, as there is mention of an inn in a conveyance when it was sold in 1683. Information in the inn says that a pub on this site had a liquor licence in the 1400s. The list of recorded licencees goes back to Elizabeth Slater in 1763. The sign shows the three legs associated with the Isle of Man. The Stanley family seized the Isle of Man in 1405 from Henry Percy, Earl of Northumberland and were granted the rights to the island and its courts. They then took the Legs of Man as their badge, when they assumed the title Lords of the Isle of Man. According to tradition the three legs indicate a willingness to kneel to England, kick at Scotland and spurn Ireland. At once time it was suggested that pubs displaying this sign meant that Manxmen were welcomed. The pub may have taken advantage of this. Information in the inn says that the name came from the nineteenth century when passengers using the Isle of Man Steamship Co. arrived in Liverpool to be conveyed to London. As the inn was on the Liverpool to London coaching route it might therefore have adopted this name to welcome passengers.

LEOPARD, Nantwich. The sign shows a red leopard placed against a white wall with the white showing through to indicate the leopard's spots.

Leather's Smithy, Macclesfield Forest.

Legs of Man, Smallwood.

THE LETTERS INN, Tattenhall. This pub originally had a sign showing letters of the alphabet. It now has a picture of a red post box.

LIMES, Sandbach. The pub has photographs of waggons made at local factories.

THE LION, Runcorn. The pub has the sign of a lion's head with a huge mane.

LION AND RAILWAY, Northwich. This pub, originally called the Lion Hotel, was built in 1860 to take advantage of the trade from the nearby station. Travellers could continue their journey by hiring horses from the stables. Until 1958 local undertakers used an upstairs room as a chapel of rest, although this did not seem to have troubled the drinkers below. The name of the first landlord Jabez Hickson can be seen on the Manchester Road gable end. The sign is an imaginative one of a rearing lion encircled by a railway track.

LION & SWAN, Congleton. The sign shows a somewhat aggressive swan with right leg and webbed foot upraised and a lion rampant, facing each other and placed in separate oval designs. The lion was a heraldic beast of the monarch and the swan was the heraldic device of the Dukes of Buckingham, Edward II, Henry IV and Edward IV. The building is one of the oldest in the town, parts of it dating back to 1650 when Roger Kent was the innkeeper. The name is perhaps a combining of two inns, in the eighteenth century, respectively called the Lion and the Swan. In the nineteenth century it was an important coaching inn on the London to Liverpool and Manchester run.

LITTLE MAN, Wettonhall. There is a figure indicating the pub name carved in stone on the front of the pub and the sign displays a little man dressed in white breeches, red waistcoat, black coat and black hat. The pub is named after a dwarf, Sammy Grice. He was a Chester man who made his living from selling meat skewers and pegs for beer barrels.

LONDON BRIDGE, Appleton. The sign depicts the bridge over the canal and the name is taken from the bridge and London Road. The pub was built in the eighteenth century alongside the Bridgwater Canal and bargemen could stable their horses here. A history of the canal has been placed on the patio.

LORD BYRON, Macclesfield. The pub displays a sign showing a variant of the portrait of the poet painted by Richard Westall in 1813. Lord Byron (1788-1824) died at Missolonghi while fighting for the Greeks in their struggle for independence from the Turks.

THE LORD CLYDE, Bollington. The sign depicts a portrait of Lord Clyde (1792-1863). Originally given the title of Sir Colin Campbell, he was a distinguished soldier whose career began in the Peninsular War. He served in China, was Lieutenant Governor of

The Letters Inn, Tattenhall.

The Lion, Runcorn.

Canada, commanded the Highland Brigade in the Crimea and played a major part in the victory gained at the Battle of Balaclava (1854). He was Commander-in-Chief of the British Army in India at the time of the Indian Mutiny and gained fame for relieving the Siege of Lucknow (1857). He was created Baron Clyde in the following year.

THE LORD COMBERMERE, Audlem. The sign depicts the head of a bearded gentleman, presumably Lord Combermere. (*See* **Bhurtpore Inn** and **Combermere Arms**.)

LORD ELDON, Knutsford. The pub was originally called the Duke of Wellington but the name was changed when the duke lost popularity when he supported the Catholic Emancipation Act (1829) and Lord Eldon opposed it. John Scott, 1st Earl of Eldon (1751-1838), was twice Lord Chancellor under a Tory government. He opposed liberal reform and in particular allowing Catholics to take public office. A small sundial is over the main door of the pub. The sign painter has made a fine effort to portray the Eldon coat of arms: argent, an anchor erect sable, between three lion heads erased gules; on a wavy chief azure, a portcullis with chains or. Crest: a lion's head erased gules, gorged with a chain and pendant these from a portcullis or. Supporters: Two lions guardant proper, each gorged with a double chain and a portcullis attached thereunto gold, pendant from the portcullis a shield argent charged with a civic wreath vert. Beneath this, the words 'Let Honour be without Shame' are a translation of the family motto *Sit sine labe decus*.

The Lord Combermere, Audlem.

LORD RODNEY, Warrington. A three-masted galleon is placed in a roundel over the main door and the windows have panes of glass depicting three-masted ships and a naval officer in eighteenth-century uniform. (*See* **Admiral Rodney**.)

THE LOWER ANGEL, Warrington. The sign shows an angel with a red and blue robe and red-feathered wings.

THE LOWER CHEQUER, Sandbach. The inn dates from 1570 and the sign shows several men, dressed in nineteenth-century clothing, gazing at a chequer board, which was used for accounting purposes. There is an abacus on the right. The pub still has a mounting block against one wall.

M

THE MARKET TAVERN, Sandbach. This pub, one of six situated around the cobbled Market Square, was originally a cycle maker and repairer's shop. The sign shows the pub with the Sandbach Crosses situated nearby. These are dated to the ninth century AD and the carvings on them represent the life and passion of Christ.

MARLBOROROUGH ARMS, Chester. This half-timbered building contains pictures of old Chester. It is said that when the painter spelt the name wrongly there was no money left to correct the spelling.

MALT SHOVEL, Neston. The sign shows a large malt shovel crossways across a wheatsheaf. Below a man shovels barley. If barley is allowed to germinate and produce shoots, it develops an enzyme, diastase, which converts grain starch into fermented sugars. To encourage this to happen, the grain is spread out, dried to convert it to malt and constantly turned, which is the action shown here. Roasting can stop the malting process, after which the crushed malt is steeped in water to produce wort, a sweet brown liquid, which is essential to produce beer.

MARQUIS OF GRANBY, Warrington. The sign shows a red-coated soldier wearing a tricorn hat and an armoured breastplate with his right hand resting on a sword. John Manners, Marquis of Granby (1721-70), son of the 3rd Duke of Rutland, was Colonel of the Royal Regiment of Horse Guards in 1758 and became Commander in Chief of the Army in 1760. He was noted for his courage in battle, often riding at the head of his troops as he did at the Battle of Warburg against the French during the Seven Years War. During one charge his wig blew off and his bald head, shining in the sun, was said to have formed a 'guiding light' for his men giving rise to the saying 'going bald-headed for it'. He was extremely popular because he provided funds for disabled senior non-commissioned officers to set themselves up as tavern keepers when they had to leave the Army at a time when no other funds were given to them. It was thus inevitable that they would name their pubs in honour of their patron.

THE MASKERY, Congleton. This is a new pub replacing a former restaurant. The name is appropriate as it is on the site of Samuel Maskery's bakery, which supplied Congleton with its famous Congleton Gingerbread in the nineteenth century. The sign, not surprisingly, depicts a Gingerbread Man.

The Maskery, Congleton.

The Maypole, Acton Bridge. *The Merlin, Leighton.*

THE MASONIC, Runcorn. This pub is nicknamed the Long Pull from the drayman's horses pulling the barrels up the steep hill by the side. Symbols carved into stones at the top of the front of the pub indicate it was once a Masonic lodge. The sign shows a shield supported by two beavers.

THE MAYPOLE, Acton Bridge. The black wrought-iron sign shows four children dancing round a maypole decked with golden ribbons. This was commonly done to celebrate May Day and the ceremony still occurs in many Cheshire villages, when the May Queen (sometimes with a May King) is crowned and led in procession to the village church.

MEMPHIS BELLE, Burtonwood. This pub was built about ten years ago on the site of the hangar in which this plane was housed. The *Memphis Belle* was a B7 Flying Fortress, a United States bomber, based at Burtonwood Airfield during the Second World War, which made many bombing raids over Germany. A documentary film was produced in 1944 of the last mission of this plane and this was re-created as a film in 1990. The pub once displayed artefacts from the airfield but these have disappeared in a recent renovation. The airbase once housed over 18,000 personnel and was a mainstay during the post-war Berlin Airlift.

THE MERCHANTS HOUSE, Macclesfield. This is a new sign for a recently built pub, which refers to the Macclesfield silk industry. It depicts a merchant standing in front of his country house with silk bobbins and coins placed on the ledge in front of him.

The Merchants House, Macclesfield.

The full bottom wig of the merchant dates him to the late-seventeenth century and the making of silk button and silk twist was established in Macclesfield by that date.

THE MERLIN, Leighton. Although the name was appropriate as it is near to the Rolls-Royce factory, which produced the Merlin engine for Spitfires during the Second World War, the present sign depicts a cartoon character of the wizard, Merlin.

MILITARY ARMS, Sandbach. The sign shows a soldier in eighteenth-century dress standing at ease holding a rifle and bayonet. Both the figure and the bayonet are moulded onto the sign. Inside the pub there are pictures of soldiers and old views of Sandbach and the pub is reputed to have a soldier ghost. The pub may refer to the story that when some Scottish troops, retreating from the Battle of Worcester in 1651, reached Sandbach, the townsfolk repulsed them. The nearby Common is still called Scotch Common.

MORRIS DANCER, Kelsall. This was previously called the Globe, and then the Olive Tree. It was a former coaching inn.

THE MOSS, Congleton. The sign shows a red-coated horseman riding a white horse at full gallop across waterlogged ground. The previous sign showed two sheep huddled on top of a dry stonewall. The name is appropriate as the pub stands on what was the edge of Mossley Moss. Until the nineteenth century many people in Congleton owned a 'moss room', that is, a strip of the moss from which they could dig peat for their fires.

Military Arms, Sandbach.

N

NAGS HEAD, various locations. A nag was a small pony. The sign is usually depicted as that of a white horse like the sign at Willaston (near Crewe) where the horse is leaning over a stable door and a similar one at Bunbury, which was a seventeenth-century coaching inn. The sign of the **Nags Head**, Willaston, Wirral, however, which was originally a school, shows the head of a brown horse. On the gable are the date 1738 and the initials RV. This possibly refers to Richard Vernon and the date when he built the house. In 1832 it was known as the Black Horse but William Delamere, a farmer and publican, revived the name of the Nags Head in 1834.

THE NARROW BOAT, Middlewich. This inn was originally called the Crown and was once used by bargemen from the nearby Trent and Mersey Canal. By the side of the inn is a cobbled way that once led to stables. The cobbles were to allow horses to get a grip on the ground. The sign shows a typical long, narrow boat making its way along a canal. Narrow boats were designed to work the narrower canals, mainly carrying coal and carting away rubbish.

THE NAVIGATION, Macclesfield and Runcorn. Both these pubs have signs showing barges on a canal. The name was applied to canals, which were dug by navigators,

Newton Brewery Inn, Middlewich.   *The Navigation, Runcorn.*

nicknamed navvies, who travelled in gangs. Pubs were often built near canals so that the navvies could use them as their headquarters, and publicans were eager that the men should spend their weekly wages there. The Macclesfield pub is near the Macclesfield Canal constructed in 1831 by James Brindley; the Runcorn one is by the side of the Bridgwater Canal.

NEWTON BREWERY INN, Middlewich. This is a popular pub by the Trent and Mersey Canal. It once had its own brewery and stabling. The sign shows a barman drawing a tankard of beer out of a barrel, while two men stand at the bar toasting each other with their tankards.

NOGGIN, Croft. A noggin can be either a pot or the small quantity of drink, which it holds. The wrought-iron sign of this pub is a sophisticated one showing in outline glasses and bottles of wine.

THE NORTON ARMS, Halton. The pub dates from 1758 and the front part was reputed to have once been a mortuary. The sign shows a white shield with a diagonal bar in blue ion which are three lozenges. Two swans act as supporters and above are a helm and a cap of maintenance with the crest of a swan.

O

THE OAKS, Knutsford. This pub used to be called the Five Oaks. The present sign shows a sprig of oak leaves with five acorns.

ODDFELLOWS ARMS, various locations. The Independent Order of Oddfellows was one of the many Friendly Societies, which were founded in the eighteenth century to assist workmen in trades in the same way as the Order of Foresters did. Its earliest meeting places were in London. Many of these had a headquarters in a pub, as that would be a place where their members would congregate. The **Oddfellows Arms**, Winsford, has the sign of a quartered shield. On the top left on a red background is an hourglass, on the top right on a blue background are crossed keys; on the lower left on a blue background is a hive and on the lower right on a red background is a lamb with a flag. These seem to cover any aspect of the Oddfellows duties. Two signs are on the **Oddfellows Arms** at Chester, one on a board, the other on the side of the wall. The signs are the same as the Winsford one except that in the centre is a shield with a thistle and a rose. The motto below is *amicitia amor et veritas* (friendship, love and truth). The **Oddfellows**, Nantwich, may have been a small theatre in the seventeenth century.

Oddfellows Arms, Chester.

OLD BARBRIDGE INN, Wardle. This pleasant pub, which sits besides the Shropshire Union Canal, has rooms called after locks.

OLD BROKEN CROSS, Rudheath. This began as a pub in 1777, the same year as the Trent and Mersey Canal was opened to traffic. It was formerly two or three cottages but these were not lined up parallel to the canal, which suggests they were built before the canal was dug. Stables were provided at the side of the pub for canal horses. The pub was intended to serve as an alehouse for watermen.

OLD CROWN, Northwich. (*See* **The Crown**.)

OLD KINGS HEAD, Macclesfield. A previous sign showing the head and crown of a medieval King indicates that this pub was called the Kings Head. The present sign represents that of a King on a playing card.

OLD HARKER'S ARMS, Chester. This was previously an early Victorian warehouse. It takes its name from a Mr Harker who used to run a chandler's shop there.

OLD MILLSTONE, Macclesfield. The sign depicts part of a millstone with some ears of corn placed partially around it. On the millstone is a mouse obviously intending to make good use of the corn.

Old Millstone, Macclesfield

OLD NAGS HEAD, Macclesfield. The sign shows a white nag's head. (*See* **Nags Head**.)

OLD QUAY HOTEL, Neston. This pub, recently renovated, overlooks what was once Gayton Sands; now grass grows alongside the quay. There are splendid views of North Wales on clear days.

OLD QUEENS HEAD, Chester, is a former coaching inn and has a sign, which imitates a portrait similar to one of Henry VIII's wives.

OLD SHIP INN, Macclesfield. The pub was converted in 1825 from a herbalist's shop. The sign is a duplicate one. On one side is a ship with three sails, its gun ports lowered to reveal the cannons. At the stern a cartoon pirate captain is waving his sword; at the bow someone is being forced to walk the plank. On the other side of the sign a UFO is blasting into space.

OLD SHIP, Styal. In spite of the somewhat battered sign, which shows a ship of the line such as fought in the Battle of Trafalgar (1805), the pub was originally named after a shippon, a farm building used to store manure. It gained its name when the farmer started brewing beer for sale.

OLDE COTTAGE, Chester. The sign shows the front of a cottage with a woman in a blue dress scrubbing the step.

THE OLDE KINGS HEAD, Sutton. The sign depicts an elderly bearded King wearing a coronet. Prince Charles Edward is said to have stayed here in 1745 on his attempt to lead his army to the conquest of England. This is a former coaching inn and smithy.

THE OX-FFORD, Macclesfield. A previous sign had the arms of the city of Oxford. The present one shows an ox with fearsome horns standing in a ford.

P

PACK HORSE, various locations. Packhorses were an efficient means of transporting goods along rough roads. They could be the sole companion of a man or travel in lines of up to forty. Inns would be a regular stopping place for the men who would need refreshment or a night's lodging. The sign of **The Pack Horse**, Broken Cross, where a red-coated man wearing a tricorn hat leads a laden donkey and a horse along a path shows just how burdened these animals could be. Perched somewhat perilously

Old Queens Head, Chester.

The Olde Kings Head, Sutton.

on top of the pack is a bucket. **The Pack Horse** at Culcheth, situated by the side of the church, shows a horse also heavily laden with its master walking by its side. These horses were used to carry loads on carefully recognised ways across Chat Moss. (*See* **Chat Moss Hotel**.)

PARR ARMS, Grappenhall. The pub, situated near the church, was the rectory in the early nineteenth century. The arms of the Parr family, a local family who founded Parr's Bank, are above the door. These are a shield argent, three bars azure surrounded by a bordure. Above is a helm. The motto is *faire sans dire* (to act without speaking). Parr's Bank was later taken over by the National Westminster Bank. On the outside of the church is a grinning animal, which may have inspired Lewis Carroll's version of the Cheshire cat.

PEACOCK, Willaston (near Crewe). This renovated inn shows a stylised sign of a peacock with tail outspread.

PEAR TREE INN, Burtonwood. The pub, dated to 1883, was originally Colliers Farm, but the name was changed and a pear tree remains close by. The sign displays a pear tree.

PENNY BLACK, Northwich. This large and restored black and white timbered pub was originally the post office. The sign is therefore appropriate as it shows the penny black stamp, the first stamp to be issued by the Royal Mail during Queen Victoria's reign, in 1840. This was an invention of Sir Rowland Hill (1795-1879), which led to the introduction of pre-paid post. The building still has the royal coat of arms at the front indicating it once received the Royal Mail.

PENNY FERRY, Latchford, Warrington. The name is taken from the cost of a journey on the ferry across the nearby canal.

THE PHEASANT INN, Burwardsley. The sign shows a pheasant, standing proudly but keeping a wary watch. Behind it in the background is Beeston Castle. The pub, situated near the Cheshire Workshops and dating back to the seventeenth century, contains many photographs and drawings of pheasants. It was originally a farm as well as a pub and there are splendid views across the Cheshire Plain from here. From the terrace, using the telescope thoughtfully provided, can be seen the two Liverpool cathedrals. In the eighteenth-century the pub was known as the Leches Arms and then became the Carden Arms, after the original owners, the Leches family of Carden Park. The Wharton family kept the pub through three generations from 1840-1928. In 1980 the pub was renamed the Pheasant. The pheasant is a game bird, raised specifically for sport, and is a popular food in Cheshire. The season is from 1 October to 1 February and it is amusing to see how the birds seem to know this, boldly strutting in the hedgerows outside these dates.

The Pack Horse, Broken Cross.

The Pack Horse, Culcheth.

Parr Arms, Grappenhall.

THE PIED BULL, Chester. This is the oldest licensed house in Chester. The site was first recorded in 1155 when Richard the Butler granted land to the nuns of St Mary's. The first innkeeper who is mentioned is Richard Grimsditch in 1571. The pub still retains the low small rooms of a sixteenth- to seventeenth-century building although the front was refurbished in the eighteenth century and the upper floors were carried out over the footpath on three segmental arches. Two ghosts are reputed to haunt the building. A man has been seen in the cellar although he occasionally makes a visit to read a newspaper in the residents' lounge. A young woman in a long dress and a white mobcap has been seen in rooms 7, 8 and 9. The pub was an important coaching inn and may have been where the novelist, George Borrow, stayed on a visit to Chester in 1862. He was given Cheshire cheese, from which he recoiled: 'to my horror the cheese had much the appearance of soap of the commonest kind, which, indeed I found it much resembled in taste, on putting a small portion into my mouth'. He had no hesitation in opening a window and 'ejecting the half-masticated morsel into the street.' He did exactly the same thing after taking a sup of ale. The inn, however, he deemed, 'pretty comfortable.'

PLOUGH, various locations. The **Plough** at Chistleton is close to the former gallows site, so it is no wonder it is reputed to be haunted. **The Plough**, Croft, was originally a spinning mill. **The Plough**, Eaton near Congleton has a fine sign on the nearby green showing two horses pulling a plough, with a 3-D plough placed over it. The pub was a farmhouse in the early seventeenth century.

The Pied Bull, Chester.

PLUMBERS ARMS, Chester. This 300-year-old pub has a punning sign showing the tools of the trade.

POACHERS INN, Bollington. This was originally called the Masonic Arms but the present name is more suited to a country district. The sign depicts a man with a brown coat and black leggings, aiming a gun while his white dog sets off in search of the spoil.

POSTERN GATE TAVERN, Warrington. This is a modern pub, which was built on the site of an old friary. A postern gate was a rear entrance where alms were handed out.

PRINCE OF WALES, various locations. This is a popular sign in the county as the Prince of Wales also has the title of Earl of Chester. Most signs like that at Crewe show three feathers. These are sometimes banded at the bottom by a gold coronet like the ones at Macclesfield and Warrington. The Macclesfield pub also has the device placed on the windows and on a mosaic to the left of the door, made by the landlady; other mosaics are at the back. Usually under the feathers are the words *ich dien*. The feathers and the motto are the insignia of the Prince of Wales. Edward, Prince of Wales (1330-1376), known as the Black Prince, adopted the feathers and this distinctive motto, '*Ich dien*' (I serve), after the Battle of Poitiers in 1356. In the sixteenth century the three single feathers were grouped into one device being bound at the bottom. The eldest

Poachers Inn, Bollington.　　　　　　　　　　　Puss in Boots, Macclesfield.

son of the monarch has been invested with the title Prince of Wales since Edward I presented his son, later Edward II, to the Welsh princes at Caernarfon in 1301, saying, rather ambiguously, that he was giving them a prince who could not speak a word of English. This was true as the prince was one year old. The present Prince of Wales was invested in Caernarfon castle in 1969. The previous sign of the **Prince of Wales**, Congleton, showed a portrait of Edward VII as Prince of Wales. This was then replaced by a splendid sign of the three feathers. Unfortunately a board with the rather boring words 'The Last Drop' has now replaced this.

PRINCES FEATHERS, Winsford. The sign shows the three feathers held at the bottom by a coronet. (*See* **Prince of Wales**.)

PUSS IN BOOTS, Macclesfield. Although the sign depicts the striding, swashbuckling figure of the fairy-tale cat, there seems no logical reason why this former coaching inn by the Macclesfield Canal should have received this name. It was adapted as a canal pub when the canal was dug in the 1830s. The sealed up arches in the gable wall once gave access to stabling for the horses pulling the canal boats. The tale of Puss in Boots (*Le Chat Botté*) was first known in Italy in the fifteenth century. From there it travelled to France and was incorporated by Charles Perrault into his fairy stories. The cat befriends a young penniless miller, claiming him to be the Marquis of Carrabas and so deceives everyone that the miller manages to marry a King's daughter.

Q

QUEENS ARMS, Bosley. This pub was a coaching house on the Macclesfield to Leek road. The sign has now been removed but it depicted a portrait of Elizabeth I dressed in coronation robes, with a cloak edged and collared with ermine, holding a sceptre in the right hand and an orb in the left. It was obviously based on the official coronation portrait of 1558. **Queens Arms**, Winsford. This is a new pub, which replaces a Victorian one.

QUEENS HEAD, various locations. The name was used during Elizabeth I's reign but became very popular during the long reign of Queen Victoria. The sign of the **Queens Head**, Congleton, depicts what purports to be the penny black stamp of Queen Victoria's reign. (*See* **Penny Black**.) **The Queens Head**, Frodsham, originally called the Kings Head, has a sign, which may represent a medieval queen. This was formerly the court leet, a manor court at which petty offences were tried. A pub was obviously the place at which to hold minor trials. It was said that murderers were hanged on the gallows at rear of the building. Part of the pub housed cotton in the eighteenth century for cotton manufacture. In the nineteenth century the parish council met in a room at the rear. Later the pub became the meeting place of the Brothers and Friendly Society of Frodsham. The former sign of the **Queens Head**, Macclesfield, displayed a portrait of Queen Victoria in her old age.

R

RAILWAY, various locations. Many of these public houses were built near stations to serve railway travellers or changed their name after 1835 when the railways began to be constructed. Railway companies took the opportunity to unite Cheshire towns, although there is still a problem as few lines run from east to west in Cheshire. Several former lines are now walking or cycling tracks. Many Cheshire pub signs, like The **Railway Inn** at Helsby, show a steam engine. **The Railway** at Barrow (now called **The Foxcote**) dates from the 1700s and was originally a cottage farmhouse. There are panoramic views across the countryside. **The Railway** at Congleton dates from 1830 and was originally called the Navigation as it was placed by the Macclesfield Canal. When the station on the North Staffordshire Railway opened in 1849, the enterprising publican, James Worth, immediately changed the name of the pub. The interior is decorated with photographs and other memorabilia relating to the

Queens Head, Congleton.

The Queens Head, Frodsham.

The Railway, Mobberley.

nearby station. **The Railway**, Mobberley, with its two signs, an engine puffing steam and a steam engine drawing its carriages, was originally part of a mill. **The Railway**, Nantwich, has ditched its sign and railway theme as the sign shows a cartoon version of the Beatles.

RAILWAY VIEW INN, Macclesfield. Created from two cottages, and situated by the side of the Manchester-London line, this pub has Stephenson's *Rocket* on its sign. The *Rocket*, built by George Stephenson in 1829, competed in the Rainhill trials for £500 offered by the Liverpool & Manchester Railway for the fastest and most reliable engine over a stated distance. The *Rocket*, painted black and yellow, won at a speed of 42kmph (26mph).

RAMS HEAD, various locations. A ram's head is the badge of the Worshipful Company of Clothworkers, but it may have a more local connotation, as it was the crest of the Leghs of Lymm. The **Rams Head**, Grappenhall, once had a splendid sign of the animal's head with huge curving horns. This has been replaced by a ram's head outlined in gold. Its 1898 porch is supported on two large pillars with Tuscan capitals. The previous sign of **The Rams Head**, Congleton, showed a somewhat quizzical ram with enormous horns looking towards the right; the present sign merely has a ram's head outlined in gold.

Railway View Inn, Macclesfield.

RAVEN INN, Glazebury, said to have been built about 1562, was part of the Holcroft estate and originally called the Holcroft Arms. The name was changed to accommodate a local legend. The story is that when a raven found the body of a soldier killed during the Civil War, it plucked out a sword from the body and took it to the roof of the pub. The sign shows a raven perched on a branch of a tree.

THE RED ADMIRAL, Warrington. This modern pub has the sign showing this species of butterfly.

RED CAT, Greasby. This was originally the New Inn which, when rebuilt, took its name from a sandstone corbel which represents a lion's head from the nearby St Hugh's Chapel built in 1398. It is these features that give rise to the mythological Cheshire Cat. (*See* **Cheshire Cat**.)

RED COW, Knutsford. The pub was called the Brown Cow, and then it became the Post Chaise, before getting its present name. It was noted for serving hearty breakfasts to farm workers.

RED LION, various locations. This is one of the most common signs for pubs. It was the badge of John of Gaunt (1340-99), fourth son of Edward III, created Duke of Lancaster in 1362, who unofficially ruled for his senile father for the latter part of the King's reign and the minority of his nephew Richard II. Parts of Cheshire were

Red Lion, Hartford.

incorporated into the Duchy and this may be one reason why the Red Lion became a popular inn sign in England. The duke's unpopularity contributed to the 1381 Peasant's Revolt when his home, the Savoy Palace in London was destroyed. The Red Lion may also be a heraldic reference to James VI of Scotland, who, on inheriting the English throne, became James I of England in 1603. He then incorporated the red lion of Scotland into the royal coat of arms and it became politic to put the heraldic red lion of Scotland on inn signs. The sign is usually displayed as a spirited lion rampant (on its hind legs). The **Red Lion**, Holmes Chapel, was originally a coaching inn. In 1692, when Peter Yates was the licensee, it was described as having good store of stabling, good cellarage and a large garden. It was occupied by highlanders in 1745, who marched south in the army of Prince Charles Edward Stuart. One scratched a prayer on a first floor window, which can still be seen. It was one of only four buildings to escape the great fire of Holmes Chapel in 1753. The **Red Lion**, Little Budworth, is the meeting point for racing drivers using Oulton Park. The **Red Lion**, Malpas is said to date from the thirteenth century and to have once been visited by James I. It was certainly a coaching inn on the London to Liverpool route and was first modernised in the 1920s. Possibly Handel stayed in the **Red Lion**, Parkgate, in April 1742, after his stay at Chester, when he was about to take ship to Dublin to give the first performance of *Messiah*. He may, however, have stayed at the George Inn, now part of the independent Mostyn Hall School, which occupies a prominent position on the estuary front. Nelson and Lady Hamilton are said to have stayed at the Red Lion. Parkgate was once an active port on the west coast for sailings to Ireland. Situated on the former quay of this busy port, the pub now overlooks the silted-up estuary. The **Red Lion**, Tarvin, was the first coaching inn from Chester on the London route; other coaching inns are **The Red Lion**, Doddleston, dating to 1640, and the **Red Lion**, Wybunbury. Two of its stables have been converted, one into a billiard room and the other a dining room. There is an elaborate portico with Doric capitals. The **Red Lion**, Hartford, differs from those displaying a heraldic sign by having a sign showing a red lion gazing across the African veldt. The **Red Lion**, Lower Withington, was rebuilt in 1899 from a previous pub, which had incorporated farm buildings; it was further extended in 1921. The **Red Lion**, Goostry, dates from the seventeenth century. The **Red Lion**, Bollington, was converted from a house by combining four rooms to make the bar. It is filled with photographs of old Bollington. The **Red Lion**, Chester, over 300 years old, has its first floor jutting out over the pavement, similar to that of the Pied Bull with which it adjoins.

THE RIFLEMAN, Winsford, has a sign showing a soldier of a Rifle Regiment in green uniform as worn in the early nineteenth century. Riflemen were founded as part of the Light Infantry during the war against America in the 1750s when General Wolfe decided that specially trained men with rifles could move quickly in forest areas without waiting for words of command. Battalions of Rifle Corps were formed after 1797 and wore dark green uniforms, adapted from those of Austrian soldiers who wore such uniforms because they blended into forest areas. They are, therefore, the first attempt at camouflage. The **Rifleman's Arms**, Wilmslow, displays an interesting sign of four soldiers, not of a Rifle Regiment as they wear red tunics, advancing with rifles at the ready. In front is an Army backpack; on it are four powder pouches and crossed rifles. **The Rifleman's Arms**, Nantwich, was once a farmhouse.

RING 'O' BELLS, various locations. Pubs of this name are often near the local church and were used by bell-ringers. **The Ring 'O' Bells**, Daresbury, which has a sign of two bells, incorporated the former Court House. Inside is the Sessions Room, renovated in 1999. On one wall are copies of the lower part of a window in the nearby church, which show characters from the story of *Alice in Wonderland*. The Revd Charles Dodgson (Lewis Carroll, 1832-98) was vicar here before he moved to Oxford. The **Ring 'O' Bells**, Stretton, was converted from a row of cottages in the nineteenth century. The sign shows an upturned bell with a prominent clapper as if taking part in a peal. The **Ring 'O' Bells**, Widnes, does not display the original sign, which was taken down a few years ago. This displayed a bear being followed by a man with a hand bell to warn passers-by and may have referred to the custom of bear-baiting so prevalent in Cheshire. The present sign depicts a man in eighteenth-century costume running away from a church with his fingers pushed in his ears. Upstairs are stained glass windows taken from a nearby Roman Catholic church. Three tunnels were found under the building, which were reputed to be escape routes for Roman Catholic priests who might be caught celebrating Mass.

The Rifleman, Winsford.

Ring 'O' Bells, Stretton.

The Rising Sun, Scholar Green.

RISING SUN, various locations. This was the badge of Edward II and Richard, Duke of York, later Richard III, but in country areas it more likely depicted a rising sun, which heralded the day's work. There is a fine sign of a cock greeting a smiling sun rising over the English countryside at **The Rising Sun**, Scholar Green. The sign of the **Rising Sun**, Tarporley, has a cock set against an enormous rising sun. The **Rising Sun** at Rainow has views across the Cheshire Plain. It was converted in 1834 from a row of cottages.

ROBIN HOOD, Rainow, was originally the village smithy, and dates back at least 200 years. It was previously called the Robin Hood and Friar Tuck. **Robin Hood** Buglawton. This building probably dates from the eighteenth century. A stone in the pub wall, dated 1787, commemorates the building as being a court for Buglawton. This was probably a court leet which dealt with such matters as transfer of land, rentals and problems relating to other countryside matters. A previous sign shows Robin discharging an arrow. The present sign depicts an incident in the life of this famous outlaw. When Robin tried to cross over a log bridge crossing a river, he was opposed by Friar Tuck, who knocked him into the stream. Robin lies in the stream, looking at his opponent who later joined his band of outlaws. **The Robin Hood**, Helsby, has a somewhat similar sign. Robin Hood first appeared in William Langland's *Vision of Piers Plowman* (1377) as a former archer. He was

Robin Hood, Buglawton.

later said to be either Robin of Locksley or Robin Fitzooth, Earl of Huntingdon, who was driven from his lands by an unscrupulous Sheriff of Nottingham. He was also said to live in Sherwood Forest where he robbed the rich to give to the poor, making his exploits very popular with that group of people in the medieval period. There is unfortunately no definite evidence that this historical or mythical outlaw, the 'wish-fulfilment protector of the medieval villeins' as he has been called, ever visited Cheshire. An old English ballad, however, mentioned Robin in connection with Ranulph, Earl of Chester, who owned Macclesfield Forest, and also Will Scarlett, a prominent member of Robin's band of outlaws. The ballad said that Will was born and dwelt in Maxfeld (Macclesfield) Town. To confuse the issue, Ranulph was Earl of Chester in the thirteenth century, whereas the ballads date to the fourteenth century.

ROEBUCK, various locations. A roebuck is the male of the roe deer. **The Roebuck**, Mobberley, with a sign showing this deer, dates to the early eighteenth century. The **Roebuck**, Northwich, with a sign showing the deer, was built about 1720 and is probably the oldest pub in Northwich, as it became an alehouse seven years later. It was probably converted from three cottages, and was extended several times. Additional stabling for horses was provided. There once was a well at the rear, which the local magistrates ordered should be sealed in 1898.

Romping Donkey, Hassall Green.

ROMPING DONKEY, Hassall Green. The pub, by the side of the Macclesfield Canal, has a sign showing a donkey kicking up its heels.

ROSE AND CROWN, various locations. The sign first became popular in the sixteenth century and was probably a wise move to indicate that the publican owned loyalty to the monarchy. Henry VII had won his throne at the Battle of Bosworth in 1485 but as his lineal descent to the throne was somewhat dubious, he had to legitimise it. This he did by marrying Elizabeth of York, daughter of Henry VI, whose beauty had given her the appellation of the Rose of York. The crown of England (Henry) and his connection with the red rose of Lancaster was thus forever coupled with the white rose of York (Elizabeth) and symbolised the end of the Wars of the Roses (1455-71). The **Rose and Crown**, Allgreave, with its inn sign of a stylised white and red rose placed below an equally stylised crown, set the pattern for pseudo-picturesque inn signs. The pub is situated in scenic countryside in the Cheshire Peak District. The sign of the **Rose and Crown**, Congleton, has the white rose, imposed on a red rose, both set within a golden coronet.

ROUNDHOUSE, Weston. This pub takes its name from its curved front and is nicknamed the Top House because of its location. It contains cartoons of local characters.

ROYAL, Runcorn. This is now regrettably called The Last Orders. It is reputed to be the oldest pub in the town and got its name because William of Orange is reputed to have stayed here on his way to Ireland, where he defeated a Catholic force under the deposed King James II in 1690. The original hostelry is now the front lounge.

ROYAL OAK, various locations. The sign became popular after the Restoration of Charles II in 1660. The King, together with a companion, Colonel Carless, had hidden in an oak tree near Boscobel House in Shropshire in order to escape from his enemies after the Battle of Worcester in 1651. He then made his way to the south coast of England, and thence to France, with the help of members of the Lane family. When the King returned, it was decreed that the 29 May should be celebrated as Oak Apple Day or Royal Oak Day in memory of the King's survival. The **Royal Oak** (now **The Oak**) at Kelsall with its sign of a crown against an oak is opposite the village lockup. The **Royal Oak**, Worleston, a former coaching inn, is one of the few in the county to display a sign. Here a crown is placed against the leaves of an oak tree. The **Royal Oak**, Macclesfield (now renamed) once had a sign showing the King hiding in the tree while his enemies searched below. This pub then became HMS Royal Oak taking its name from the battleship the *Royal Oak* that was sunk in 1939 at Scapa Flow in the Orkneys.

Royal Oak, Worleston.

Ryles Arms, Langley.

ROYAL OAK BRANCH, Warrington, has a sign showing the head of Charles II, set within a roundel, placed on the branch of a tree where it meets the trunk.

RYLES ARMS, Langley. The pub was named after a local landowner who opened the first bank in Macclesfield. It was originally a forge where token coins were minted. The sign appears to be an imaginative one with in chief two horses above a Staffordshire knot; below quarterly are first and fourth two lions rampant gules, second an eagle with wings outspread and in third a harp.

S

THE SALAMANCA, Smallwood. The pub (now closed) stood on the site of four cottages owned by Sir Stapleton Cotton (*See* **Combermere Arms** and **Bhurtpore Inn**), and the houses were probably converted into a pub to give employment to one of his retired soldiers. The sign showed British troops dressed in uniforms of the early nineteenth century period heavily engaged in the battle, probably the Battle of Salamanca (1812) during the Peninsular War, in which the Duke of Wellington defeated the French forces.

SALT BARGE, Marston. This was built to replace the Townsend Arms, which closed in 1913 and sank into the waters of the 'flashes' caused by water gathering over collapsed mines. The sign shows one of the barges, which carried salt. The pub is a useful venue for visitors to the Lion Salt Works. On the other side of the canal bridge is one of the larger 'flashes', which covers the site of the Marston Mine.

SANDPIPER, Sandwich. The pub displays a sign of the bird, which is usually found on marshy ground or on inland waters such as reservoirs.

SARACEN'S HEAD, various locations. A Saracen was a person of Arab descent, which came to mean Muslim. The Crusaders used it as a heraldic device and many of them, on their return to England, included a Saracen's head in their coat of arms. Medieval archers also used a Saracen's head as a practice target and they usually had their butts near to pubs so that they could seek refreshment later. It thus became a popular inn sign either as a tribute to the local lord or from the archery ground. The **Saracen's Head**, Warburton, dates from the seventeenth century and has a 3-D sign of a Saracen's Head. Dick Turpin is said to have stayed here. The **Saracen's Head**, Warrington has a painted sign showing the head of a man wearing a red turban.

SETTER DOG, Walker Barn, Rainow. This pub was built about 1740 and is a great favourite with walkers in the Peak District. It originally served as a post office.

SHAKERLEY ARMS, Congleton. The sign reproduces the arms of the Shakerley family: argent a chevron between two hillocks or mole hills vert. Crest: a hare proper resting its fore feet on a garb or. The Shakerley family originated in Lancashire and moved to Cheshire in the sixteenth century and became active in the history of the county. Sir Peter Shakerley (1763-1859) moved to Somerford Hall near Congleton in 1838. In the nineteenth century, Sir Walter Shakerley, the Lord of the Manor of Congleton, was a noted benefactor of the town. One of his most generous gifts was presenting land in 1871 for a public park, which has recently been revitalised with Lottery Heritage money. The pub was called the Black Rabbit in the mid-nineteenth century, a name which may derive from the hare in the Shakerley crest.

SHADY OAK, Tiverton. The pub is near Beeston Castle and on the side of the Shropshire Union Canal.

SHIP, Chester. The name comes from its use by fishermen on the River Dee. The pub contains artefacts of the Cheshire Regiment. **The Ship Inn**, Wincle. This pub, converted from three cottages, is very popular with walkers. The inn was probably built in the sixteenth century although Joshua Cundy is the first known landlord from 1749-88. Later it came into the possession of the Brocklehursts of Swythamley Hall. The Ship is named after a Liverpool vessel, named *Swythamley*, which was owned by a close friend of the local squire of Swythamley and foundered off the Cape of

Above and right: *The Ship Inn, Wincle.*

The Ship Hotel, Parkgate.

The Ship Victory, Chester.

Good Hope in 1862. In 1745, a man, believed to be a highlander from the army of Prince Charles Edward Stuart, held up the innkeeper and his family and demanded his gun. He departed leaving behind his own musket. The present sign has two scenes: one shows a ship trapped in the ice with two men hauling a sledge towards it; the other has the arms of the Brocklehurst family. This contains in two of the four quarters three brocks or badgers. There is also a badger as a crest. John Brocklehurst, a silk worker, bought and rebuilt Swythamley Hall in 1813. His grandson, Sir Philip, sailed with Ernest Shackleton on his expedition to the Antarctic during 1908-09. The picture on the sign of a ship, enclosed in ice, is of the Nimrod, which Shackleton used on this expedition. In 1938 Sir Philip's younger brother, who lived at Roach House near the Roaches, introduced wallabies into his private zoo. Some escaped and until about fifteen years ago could be seen living wild in the area. **The Ship**, Style, although having a sign showing a ship of the line similar to one which fought at the Battle of Trafalgar (1805), was originally a shippon, a farm building for cattle or sheep. **The Ship Hotel**, Parkgate, has a sign showing a three-masted vessel and is a reminder that this small village was once a busy port.

THE SHIP VICTORY, Chester. The name of this pub is unique. The sign shows a ship with three sails and on each is written one of the pub's names. The pub was named after Nelson's ship, which won the Battle of Trafalgar in 1805. Inside are etchings and paintings of the ship. One sign shows a painting of the ship dated to 1759 but the keel of the ship was laid down in 1765. Manchester City football supporters, who gather here before and after their team's matches, use the pub as a rendezvous.

SHREWSBURY ARMS, Little Budworth, was built in 1880. The **Shrewsbury Arms**, Mickle Trafford, was part of the estate of the Earl of Shrewsbury, which was sold in 1917. It was then known as the Shrew and was one of sixty-eight lots parcelled up for the auction. It was let to the Cheshire Brewery for £90 a year. It was one of the haunts of highwaymen in the eighteenth century. On 6 April 1796 Thomas Brown and James Price tied up and robbed a fifteen-year-old mail boy. The lad freed himself and ran to the tollhouse opposite to seek help. The robbers were caught in Birmingham, brought back to Mickle Trafford to be tried and hanged in Gibbet Field. The Talbot family was mentioned in Domesday Book and the Earldom of Shrewsbury dates back to 1442 when Sir John Talbot, who had fought bravely in the wars against France, was elevated to the peerage. The Earldom of Talbot was created in 1784 and in 1856 on the death of the 17th Earl of Shrewsbury, the 3rd Earl Talbot succeeded to both earldoms. It became linked with the earldom of Talbot in the nineteenth century. The coat of arms is quarterly first and fourth a lion rampart within a bordure engrailed or; second and third azure a chevron between three mullets or. There are two crests one for Shrewsbury and one for Talbot. The supporters, not surprisingly, are two silver talbots. The motto is *prest d'accomplis* (ready for action).

THE SHROPSHIRE ARMS, Chester. The sign shows the arms of the county, erminois, three piles azure, two issuant from the chief and one in base, each charged with a leopard's face. The motto on the sign is *fioriat Salopia* but the correct one should be *floriat Salopia*.

THE SHROPPIE FLY, Audlem. The building, originally constructed as a canal warehouse, was closed in 1970. It underwent restoration and emerged as a public house lying alongside the Shropshire Union Canal. The name comes from the term 'fly boats', elite barges, which were intended to carry passengers and goods more swiftly along the canal than cargo boats. They sailed non-stop both day and night with a strict timetable, which separated them from other canal traffic. Their four-man crew could change horses on the move. The sign shows the stern of a fly boat with a man at the helm and two other men standing on the deck. An original shroppie fly boat is incorporated into the bar of the pub. Drinkers at the pub watch with interest the efforts of the boaters as they negotiate one of the fifteen locks on the canal, which raise the boats 28m (93ft) from the Cheshire Plain to Shropshire.

SIR ROBERT, Ellesmere Port. The pub commemorates Sir Robert O'Loyd, a local builder. It contains mementoes of Liverpool and Everton football clubs.

THE SMOKER, Plumley. The sign depicts Lord de Tabley on his horse, called The Smoker. The pub is a sixteenth-century building, which has been altered several times. The first Lord de Tabley raised the Cheshire Yeomanry to defend the country against an invasion by Napoleon. His white (or smoky grey) charger was bred as a racehorse by the Prince Regent and the inn was named as a memorial to the horse.

Spinner & Bergamot, Combermere.

A painting in the dining room at Tabley Hall shows Lord de Tabley on this horse reviewing his troops on the beach at Liverpool. The racing calendar of 1790-93 records that The Smoker won twelve out of nineteen races, was second out of three races and was third or unplaced for only two. A cup won by The Smoker in 1792 was given to the Tarporley Hunt Club and is now presented as a challenge cup in Cheshire point-to-point races.

SPINNER & BERGAMOT, Cambermere. The names refer to two horses in the eighteenth century, whose heads, one white and one brown, are both depicted on the sign. They were owned by the Honourable John Smith Barry of Marbury Hall. A bergamot is a tree but it is also the name given to a kind of tapestry made from flock and the hair of goats or oxen. It was produced in Bergamo in Italy, hence the name, but it may also have been made in the village. This pub has a collection of horse brasses.

SPINNERS ARMS, Bollington. The sign usually relates to the cotton trade. The sign shows a fisherman holding a large fish and presumably about to spin a tale. The cotton trade is not forgotten and in the rear is a mill and the words [Y]ARN [SP]INNERS can be made out on its side.

SPORTSMANS ARMS, Tattenhall. This was a rendezvous for horse dealers from Whitchurch. The sign shows a mounted huntsman blowing his horn with his hounds gathered round him.

Sportsmans Arms, Tattenhall.

SPREAD EAGLE, Lymm. An eagle with wings outspread is often seen on coats of arms as a heraldic device, especially by families who had travelled abroad, where the eagle is commonly used as this device. This pub, however, has two different signs: a painted one showing an eagle hovering above a snowy mountainous landscape and a 3-D brass eagle mounted on a ball. A similar object was often designed as a reading lectern in churches being a symbol of St John the Apostle who was the author of the fourth Gospel.

STAFFORDSHIRE KNOT, Congleton. This sign is more usually found in Staffordshire. It was a device on the arms of the Barons of Stafford and became the cap badge of both the South Staffordshire Regiment, raised in 1702 as the 38th Foot, and the North Staffordshire Regiment, raised as the 64th Foot in 1768. The South Staffs had the knot surmounted by a crown and the North Staffs a knot surmounted by the Prince of Wales feathers. The two regiments amalgamated to form the Staffordshire Regiment and are now a battalion in the Mercian Regiment. Tim Carew's book, *How the Regiments got their Nicknames*, comments that the 38th Foot was sent to keep order in Antigua in 1706. Newly formed and far away, it was allowed to languish there for the next sixty years. Its uniforms became so threadbare that they were constantly patched with brown Holland cloth. George V awarded the regiment the right to wear a piece of this material behind the cap badge as a reminder of that time. This became known as the Staffordshire knot. Another story, however, points to it being an economical knot, which was said to have been devised by three brothers, who, sentenced to death after being caught poaching, preferred to hang at the same time.

Stanley Arms, Chester.

STANLEY ARMS, Anderton. The name refers to the owners of Winnington Hall. The coat of arms above the door represents those of the Stanley family who are descended from Adam de Stanley in the time of Henry II. Thomas, Lord Stanley was created Earl of Derby at the coronation of Henry VII in 1485. He had been a supporter of Richard III but realising where power ultimately lay, had switched to Henry Tudor's side at the Battle of Bosworth, thus ensuring Henry's victory. This pub is known as 'The Tip' because salt and debris from nearby workings were tipped into canal barges outside the pub, which is near to the Anderton Boat Lift, opened in 1876 to lift barges between the River Weaver and the Trent and Mersey Canal. It stands on the site of the stables, which once housed the canal barge horses. The **Stanley Arms**, Chester, has a sign showing the coat of arms of the family. The Stanley family had a town house in Chester in Watergate Street. The Stanley coat of arms are incorporated into those of the Earls of Derby; argent, on a bend azure three stag's heads cabossed or. The crest is on a chapeau gules, an eagle with wings extended or, preying on an infant in its cradle. Supporters are a griffin and a stag. The motto is *sans changer* (unchanging). (*See* **Eagle and Child**.) **The Stanley Arms**, Langley, set in wild countryside, was originally a farmhouse. It was called the Derby Arms after Lord Derby but the name was changed during the Second World War to the Derby family name of Stanley. There was once a wooden hut, reputed to be the original changing room of the jockeys at Aintree, serving as a tearoom in the car park. Even though this has been moved to Tor Gate farm, the pub is very popular with walkers. (*See* also **Legs of Man**.)

STAR, Acton. The sign shows a star shining in a dark night. The timber-framed building dates back to 1590. **The Star**, Statham, Lymm, is a seventeenth-century farmhouse which had an extension built on to serve the navvies who built the Bridgwater Canal.

STATION, Ellesmere Port. The sign shows the station and a steam engine, and like many of pubs relating to the railway, the sign favours a steam engine above a modern engine. The pub contains items of railway interest.

STRETTON FOX, Stretton. The cartoon sign depicts a smirking fox sitting up very alert by the side of two somewhat apprehensive rabbits. He has attempted to disguise himself with a rabbit's ears, a tail and protruding front teeth.

SUTTON HALL, Sutton. The pub was originally the baronial farm of the Sutton family and contains much sixteenth-century woodwork.

THE SWAN, various locations. The swan can be a heraldic device but in the Cheshire countryside relates more to the birds of the area. The **Swan Inn** at Holmes Chapel was once a farmhouse and the original yard is still entered through an arch. It became a pub when the railway arrived in 1838. The name was transferred here from a pub at Cranage, which was once a drovers' inn. The Cranage site is now Swan Farm. The **Swan**, Tarporley, with its most dignified sign of a swan out of the water and stretching its wings, is a former coaching inn. From 1769 it has been the headquarters of the Tarporley Hunt, one of the oldest in England, which meets in the Hunt Room, a room partly over a former market hall. The walls are lined with pictures of hunting scenes. **The Swan**, Winnick, has a 3-D sign with the swan perching on a post bearing the pub name. The pub, built in the seventeenth century, was originally a drinking establishment with stalls dating from 1888. **The Swan**, Wybunbury, has a sign showing

Stretton Fox, Stretton.

a swan with two cygnets. It is an eighteenth-century brick building. Fig Pudding Wakes were held in the street outside in March during the nineteenth century but the wakes were discontinued when they fell into disrepute. The tradition of Fig Pie Rolling was revived in 1995 and it was firmly established on 1 June in 2000. The pies are baked rock hard and rolled down the hill between The Swan and the Red Lion. The winner gets to keep the pie, which survives intact. The prize for the adults is a bottle of port.

SWAN & CHEQUERS, Sandbach. The building was originally built as the Swan Hotel in 1895 to replace an earlier Swan Hotel. The Chequers was added when a nearby pub was demolished.

SWAN WITH TWO NECKS, Nantwich and Macclesfield. This name dates back to at least the sixteenth century. Traditionally all swans are the property of royalty, but Elizabeth I granted both the Dyers Co. and the Vintners Co. the right to have swans. The Vintners Co. identified their swans by two nicks made on the beak. As the Vintners Co. was associated with taverns, the name was often adopted for pub signs. All the signs show a swan with two necks and this seems to have come about because a nick is an obsolete word for neck. It is also the case that it would be easier for a pub sign painter to paint two necks more dramatically and recognisable than two nicks. The Macclesfield pub was originally called The Swan Wi' Two Nicks but one of the present signs has a crown placed between the necks of the swans thus indicating they are royal property.

Swan Inn, Holmes Chapel. *Swan with Two Necks, Macclesfield.*

SWETTENHAM ARMS, Swettenham. No sign but worth mentioning for its village setting. The pub, parts of which date back to at least the fourteenth century, is believed to be on the former site of a nunnery and to have an underground passage leading to the village church. This was said to have been used by funeral corteges who stayed first at the nunnery and then at the inn and moved coffins along this passage. There is the usual story of the ghost of a nun who had broken her vows. An exorcism during the twentieth century took care of her. The pub contains the Lovell Suite, named after Sir Bernard Lovell, the astronomer who helped in the development of radar and was Director of Jodrell Bank Radio Telescope.

SWINGING WITCH, Northwich. This 200-year-old pub has now been renamed the **Crown** (*See* **Crown**.)

SYDNEY ARMS, Crewe. This was originally a nineteenth-century farmhouse. The name seems to have been derived from the local district called Sydney and is not related to a local family. Nevertheless the sign displays a dignified coat of arms: a blue shield with a wavy white line between three goat's heads. Above the shield is a helm with a goat's head crest.

T

TALBOT ARMS. A Talbot is a breed of hound used for tracking and hunting. It can be used as a heraldic device and was used by the Earls of Shrewsbury and the Talbot family who had a hound as a crest or supporters on their coat of arms. The **Talbot**, Nantwich, has a dog painted on the wall. (*See* also **The Tunnel Top**.)

TEMPLE BAR, Chester. This pub was originally called The City Arms and still bears the arms of the city of Chester, both on a sign and on the side of the upper storey. This is gules, three lions passant guardant in pale or, azure three garbs. The crest is a sword held erect with a gold hilt and pommel within a black sheath. The supporters are a lion and a wolf. The motto is *antique colant antiquam dierum*. The pub was renovated in 1892 and in 1957 the whole pub was given a complete makeover and renamed. In the rear area a pulpit and a confessional have been incorporated into the décor.

THATCHED TAVERN, Northwich. This opened as a beer-house with its premises formed from three cottages built at different dates. It has a handsome sign of the present pub and although this pub is not thatched, its predecessor had a thatched roof.

THE THORN INN, Appleton. The sign displays the thorn tree and the church. The Appleton Thorn was reputedly grafted from the Glastonbury Thorn, which grew from

The Thorn Inn, Appleton.

the staff of Joseph of Arimathea, and ceremonies were held to commemorate this. The present custom, revived in the 1970s, called 'bawming' (or adorning) the thorn with garlands and ribbons is held in June and includes a children's procession. Certain trees have been considered sacred since prehistoric times and often had articles tied to them to bring good fortune to the giver. The pub was once part of the Arley Estate. An inscription above the door reads:

> You may safely while sober sit under the thorn.
> But if you are drunk overnight it will prick you next morn.

THREE ARROWS, Congleton. The sign shows three arrows, tied with a red and gold scroll. Arrows often appear on inn signs as part of a heraldic motif created for the Worshipful Company of Fletchers, which licensed the making of arrows and controlled their quality. Butts for archery practice were often erected near to pubs so that refreshment could be obtained during and after the exercise. The pub was a coaching inn on a regular run between Birmingham and Manchester. The entrance leading to the yard and stable has now been bricked up to create a room.

THREE CROWNS, Macclesfield. The sign shows the three crowns and there are several interpretations of the name. They may have been the crowns worn by the three wise men (also called Magi or Kings) but any sign with these would become obsolete at the Reformation. When James I became King of England, the three crowns referred to the union of England, Scotland and Wales. They may also have a heraldic interpretation referring to the Worshipful Company of Drapers incorporated in 1561.

THREE GREYHOUNDS, Allostock. The sign shows three greyhounds, two standing, and one lying down, all relaxed but alert. The pub was originally a farmhouse. There is a yew tree in the garden, which is over 200 years old.

THE THREE LAMPS, Crewe. The sign shows three lamps but they do not bear any resemblance to the original lamps. The pub was originally called the Cheese Hall and then the Stilton probably because it was next to the Cheese Market, which flourished in the nineteenth century. The original three lamps were on High Town, opposite the Jubilee Gardens. They were twice relocated before finding a home outside the pub.

THREE PIGEONS, Nantwich, built around 1600. This may relate to pigeon racing, which was, and still is, a sport in the north of England. The lounge was a former butcher's shop. The bar is in the original pub. The sign of the **Three Pigeons**, Warrington, shows three birds perched on two branches of a tree.

THE TOLLEMACHE ARMS, Alpaham. This old pub was once part of estate of Lord Tollemache. (*See* also **The Beeston Castle** and **Dysart Arms**.)

TOWN CRIER, Chester. The sign shows a town crier holding a piece of parchment ready to read it. This was an official, once found in every town, who rang his bell before making official pronouncements, a vital necessity when there was no radio and few people could read. In the summer months Chester still keeps up this old custom when the Town Crier makes announcements from the Market Cross.

TRAVELLERS REST, various locations. As travelling throughout Britain increased from the sixteenth century onwards, so did the number of places offering food, company and hospitality, even if it meant sharing a bed and being bitten by fleas. This was especially necessary when monasteries, which had considered it their Christian duty to house travellers, were dissolved between 1536 and 1539. The Travellers Rest became a very popular name for a public house as it indicated the landlord's intention to provide food, drink and lodging. **The Travellers Rest,** Frodsham, has splendid views over Cheshire Plain. The **Travellers Rest**, Scholar Green, has a sign showing two men, obviously taking their rest, leaning on a bar, one dressed in a red waistcoat and green trousers. A dog rests at his feet. The other is dressed in a blue waistcoat and grey trousers. The background is of beer barrels and tankards. The **Travellers Rest**, Macclesfield, has just repainted its sign to reflect completely the satisfaction felt when reaching an inn. A large man dressed in a red coat, blue breeches and yellow stockings sits completely at ease resting in a chair. In front of him are his tankard of ale and a swag bag of food.

TUDOR ROSE, Puddington. Henry VII adopted the Tudor rose, which combines the red rose of Lancaster and the white rose of York, as a royal badge when he married Elizabeth of York. The marriage signified the joining of the houses of York and Lancaster and the ending of their quarrel, which had resulted in the Wars of the Roses. (*See* **Rose and Crown**.)

Three Greyhounds, Allostock.

The Three Lamps, Crewe.

Town Crier, Chester.

THE TUNNEL TOP, Ditton. The pub is situated above the tunnel over the Trent and Mersey Canal. It was originally called The Talbot Arms, because of the landlord, Mr Talbot, who retired aged ninety-three, a few years ago.

U

THE UNICORN, Wilmslow and Congleton. The Wilmslow pub is over 200 years old. Both the Congleton and Wilmslow signs show a rampant white unicorn with a golden mane on a blue shield. A unicorn was a mythical and legendary animal with the body of a horse, usually pure white, with a single horn growing from its forehead. In medieval literature the creature was held to symbolise virginity. Its horn, when ground, was reputed to be a cure for all medical ills, especially poisons, hence its incorporation in the arms of the Society of Apothecaries. Two unicorns were supporters on the royal arms of the Kings of Scotland and when James VI of Scotland succeeded to the throne of England as James I, he incorporated the unicorn as a supporter of the royal arms with the lion of England, thus displacing the Welsh dragon of the Tudor dynasty. Lewis Carroll describes Alice meeting a unicorn in *Alice Through the Looking Glass*. 'Do you know,' said Alice, 'I always thought that Unicorns were fabulous monsters, too. I never saw one alive before!'
'Well, now that we have seen each other,' said the Unicorn, 'if you'll believe in me, I'll believe in you. Is that a bargain?'
'Yes, if you like,' said Alice.

UNION INN, Nantwich. The union usually refers to the unification of England and Scotland (1707), although in Cheshire it could refer to the incorporation of Wales into England (1536) by Henry VIII. The pub was built as a coaching inn in the eighteenth century by a consortium of businessmen.

V

VALE INN, Bollington. This was originally the Adelphi Cotton Mill built in the 1850s by George Swindells and was later run by his two sons. Barges on the Macclesfield Canal were used to bring raw cotton from the United States and to take away finished products; later transportation was switched to the railway. The mill was closed in the 1970s.

The Unicorn, Congleton.

VERNON ARMS, Poynton. Lord Vernon provided money for building a library and reading room. The pub has now been converted to a 'plastic' pub.

THE VICTORIA, Chester. The sign shows a picture of Queen Victoria in her later years. It stands on the site of the *principia* (headquarters building) of the Roman fort and it is claimed that there has been a pub on the site since the thirteenth century. There are odd-shaped doors, low ceilings and antique settles. The oldest roof beam is said to be over 1,000 years old. The cellar is placed over the former crypt of St Peter's church and the courtyard is flagged over its graveyard. The feature known as The Rows means that the front door of the pub is entered from the Upper Row but it can also be entered from the level of the courtyard, accessed by going up Northgate Row.

VINE INN, various locations. The vine is one of the oldest pub signs indicating a house that sold alcoholic drink and is also the heraldic device of the Worshipful Company of Distillers. It was known to have been in use as early as the fourteenth century. The Romans introduced vines into Britain and winemaking was common until well into the fifteenth century. The industry then lapsed but has had a tremendous revival since the twentieth century. **The Vine**, Shavington, displays the vine as it is just producing the grapes. **The Vine Inn**, Nantwich, with its sign of a vine bearing juicy bunches of grapes, seemingly a half-timbered building, dates back only to the 1990s.

THE VOLUNTEER. The name comes from volunteers, who were raised in regiments on two occasions, the first to resist invasion by Napoleon Bonaparte in the 1790s and the second time to fight a presumed invasion of England by Napoleon III of France in 1859. They began as small units in towns and villages and were later grouped into larger administrative units. They were often raised by a local landowner or by a county

The Victoria, Chester.

The Volunteer, Northwich.

thus becoming linked to county associations. It was not until 1881 that they became component parts of regular regiments. **The Volunteer**, Northwich, has a sign showing a volunteer dressed in uniform of the early twentieth century with spiked helmet, red tunic, white collar and sleeve facings, holding a rifle with fixed bayonet.

WAGGON & HORSES, various locations. This is a most appropriate sign in a country district where it was once one of the main methods of transporting goods. The **Waggon & Horses**, Eaton near Congleton, shows two shire horses pulling a brewer's dray laden with barrels. The **Waggon & Horses**, Congleton, has a more dramatic scene with a waggon drawn by two horses laboriously making its way uphill, apparently during a storm, through a rocky landscape.

WATERGATE INN, Chester. This is next to the racecourse and is a favourite pub of racegoers. Inside are photographs of jockeys and racehorses. The sign shows a watermill rather than a watergate. Two waterwheels are turned by a huge flow of water. The River Dee formerly flowed near to the adjoining gate.

THE WATERLOO, Runcorn. The pub is named from the nearby Waterloo Bridge, but the sign shows a cavalry charge during the Battle of Waterloo (1815). The cellar is reputed to be haunted.

THE WELLINGTON, Widnes. This pub was built in 1847 and the sign shows the Duke of Wellington in military uniform. **The Wellington**, Runcorn, has a sign of the duke, in his red tunic, with folded arms, based on the Goya portrait. This is a very popular inn sign. Arthur Wellesley (1769-1852) created 1st Duke of Wellington, had a distinguished career in India before he defeated the French troops in Spain during the Peninsular War (1809-13) and at the Battle of Waterloo in 1815. He entered politics and was Prime Minister from 1828-30, but his reactionary views in opposing Parliamentary reform almost led to civil unrest. On his death he was given a grand state funeral, and is buried in St Paul's Cathedral.

WHARF INN, Congleton and **The Wharf**, Macclesfield. Both pubs are situated near the Macclesfield Canal which opened in 1831 only to lose its commercial traffic when the North Staffordshire Railway opened in 1839. Where once the pubs served bargees, they now serve people using barges for pleasure. The Congleton sign shows two bearded men, obviously bargees, strolling by the side of the canal with a wharf in the background. A previous sign showed a barge passing under a roving or 'snailly' bridge. This bridge allowed a horse towing a barge to cross from one side of the canal to the

The Waterloo, Runcorn.

The Wellington, Runcorn.

other and the bargee would shift the rope from one side of the horse's shoulder to the other. The Macclesfield sign shows a bargee guiding his barge towards a wharf. Goods are piled by the walls of a building and a barrel is being hoisted to its upper storey.

WHEATSHEAF, various locations. A wheatsheaf can be a heraldic device known as a garb and is used on many coats of arms including those of the Worshipful Company of Bakers, the Worshipful Company of Brewers and, appropriately, on the arms of Cheshire and the Dukes of Westminster. A wheatsheaf was a common sight in farming country before the introduction of the combine harvester. The **Wheatsheaf** at Dunham on the Hill was originally called the Penny Farthing. **The Wheatsheaf**, Ness, has a sign showing a large wheatsheaf, by the side of which rests a child tended over by the mother who is taking food from her shawl. In the background her husband placidly reaps the corn. The gardens at the back overlook the silted-up Dee estuary. The **Wheatsheaf**, No Mans Heath, an eighteenth-century pub, has a large wheatsheaf on its sign. **The Wheatsheaf**, Sandbach, with a splendid sign of a large wheatsheaf, was built in 1890 at the request of Lord Crewe. It provided a shuttle service for travellers to Sandbach Station. Inside a series of mirrors, strategically placed, make the interior of the pub look much larger than it actually is.

WHEELWRIGHTS ARMS, Elton. The Worshipful Company of Wheelwrights obtained its charter in 1689.

WHIPPING STOCKS INN, Over Peover. The sign shows a person standing in a pillory rather than sitting in the stocks. Both were regular punishments during the medieval period and later. A soldier who should be standing guard is lolling asleep; a young couple strolls by and a man lolls against the side of the pillory. The inn was originally the local courthouse so it is appropriate that inside the building are pictures relating to crime and punishment.

WHITE BARN, Cuddington. The name probably derives from the fact that the barn was used as a resting place by men carrying salt on their packhorses from Northwich. It was a coaching inn before serving railway travellers.

THE WHITE BEAR, Knutsford. The dramatic sign shows a polar bear sitting on its haunches amidst an arctic icy waste. The pub dates from the seventeenth century and was a coaching inn and a stopping place on the Birmingham to Liverpool and Manchester routes. It was also used by a local highwayman called Edward Higgins, who was executed in 1767. There is an attractive thatched roof with a bird on it.

WHITE HART, various locations. A white hart is a male deer. The White Hart was the heraldic badge of Richard II (1377-99) and was a popular inn sign from that period. It was a badge worn by all his followers and therefore was regarded as a sign of loyalty to the monarch. Later the name became a general name for a public house, which explains its later popularity. The **White Hart**, Warrington, has a sign showing a white hart resting on the grass within a roundel. Above is a crown.

Whipping Stocks Inn, Over Peover.

The Wheatsheaf, Sandbach.

WHITE HORSE, various locations. The white horse was a badge of the house of Hanover and became a popular sign in the eighteenth century, although it was in earlier use in the southern part of England, being associated with the Kings of Wessex and the county of Kent. Several of the London guilds incorporate it into their heraldry.

WHITE LION, various locations. A white lion was the heraldic insignia of Edward IV and also appeared on the arms of the Earls of March and the dukes of Norfolk. Almost all pubs, like the **White Lion**, Coppenhall, have a sign showing a white lion rampant. A custom at The **White Lion** Alvanley is that a newly married couple had to pass under a rope and pay a forfeit so that locals could drink their health at the pub. The pub dates from at least 1700. The **White Lion**, Barthomley, dates to around 1614 but was mainly rebuilt in the nineteenth century when it was part of the Crewe Estate. It witnessed the massacre that took place in 1643 when, during the Civil War, Royalists drove the villagers into the church, smoked them out and slaughtered them as they emerged. The **White Lion**, Childer Thorton, held cockfights in the loft. There was once a collection of watch boxes behind the bar. The **White Lion** Knutsford is a timber-fronted building dating from 1687 with a magnificent sign of a lion rampant, protruding a red tongue. **The White Lion**, Macclesfield, until 1798, was Pickford's Brewery. There is a row of cinema seats in the lounge. **The White Lion**, Weston, has recently been extended. The original timber-framed, two-storey wing dates from 1652 and is part of the former farmhouse. The **White Lion**, Winsford, displays an ironwork sign of a rampant lion holding a pole from which flies a pennant.

White Lion, Barthomley.   *White Lion, Winsford.*

WHITE SWAN. White swans occur on coats of arms such as those of the Vintners' Company, the Earls of Essex and Edward III. **The White Swan**, Great Sutton, is a former coaching inn.

WHITTON CHIMES, Northwich, has a sign showing the church.

WICKSTEAD ARMS, Nantwich. This is a seventeenth-century building. The sign, probably referring to the Battle of Nantwich (1644), depicts in the background a battle taking place and in the foreground a Roundhead and a Cavalier. The arms are a light blue shield with three garbs on a deep blue diagonal. One bird is below this and two birds above.

WILBRAHAM ARMS, Alsager, Nantwich and elsewhere. The Wilbraham family, with its many branches, has played an important role in Cheshire history dating from at least the thirteenth century. Richard de Wilbraham was Sheriff of Cheshire in 1268-69 and later other Wilbrahams held this position. The family was particularly active in the history of Nantwich. Thomas de Wilbraham (1578-1646) lived at Sweet Briar Hall in Hospital Street. His splendid monument depicting him in plate armour is in Acton church and a later Richard de Wilbraham built a house in Welsh Row. George Wilbraham provided the town with a grammar school in 1858. The **Wilbraham Arms**, Nantwich was originally called the Red Lion. It was kept by the Partridge family in the eighteenth century, who were waggoners working between Nantwich and London. It was their private house and still looks like one. The **Wilbraham Arms**, Alsager, has a sign displaying the full coat of arms of the family. This is divided quarterly indicating the arms of Wilbraham and the arms of Baker. There are two crests, one for Baker and one for Wilbraham. The motto is *in portu quies* (there is rest in port). The Baker and Wilbraham lines merged when Sir George Baker married Kathleen Frances Wilbraham, sole heiress of the Rode Hall estate in 1900 and assumed the name and arms of the family.

WILD BOAR, Wincle. The pub is home to sportsmen for clay-pigeon shooting. At one time the signboard showed a placid pig leaning over a gate chewing straw. Now it depicts a snarling wild boar, most suitable, as this is one of several areas claiming to be that in which the last wild boar in England was killed. Today, however, wild boars have been reintroduced into England and are farmed and prized for their meat.

WILLEY MOOR LOCK TAVERN, Tarporley. This former lock-keeper's cottage is on the Llangollen Canal. The family room was originally the stables.

THE WILSONS, Runcorn. This 300-year-old building used to be called the Bowling Inn. In 1805 Joe Wilson took over the license, hence the name. The upper floors are said to be haunted by a dashing young cavalier. The sign shows a swaggering cavalier, dressed in brown, with high thigh boots and with his hand resting on his sword. The style of painting is reminiscent of the Dutch School.

THE WINDMILL, Tabley. A previous sign represented a scene from Cervantes novel *Don Quixote* where the knight charges to attack windmills thinking them to be giants. Windmills were common in England until the nineteenth century, being erected to grind corn and to pump water. The present sign shows a racehorse and rider. **The Windmill Inn**, Whitely Green, Adlington, a former farmhouse, is reputed to date from 1784, displays a sign showing a traditional windmill.

THE WIZARD OF EDGE, Alderley Edge. A previous sign over the door showed a wizard by the side of a farmer struggling with the reigns of a rearing white horse. The pub was then called The Wizard. The present sign reflects the name. Legend has it that a farmer was crossing the Edge to sell his white horse at Macclesfield market. He was stopped by an old man who asked the farmer to sell him the horse. The farmer refused whereupon the wizard said that the farmer would not sell his horse that day. This came true. No one made a bid at the market and as the farmer was making his way home he met the wizard again. This time the farmer was willing to sell the horse. The wizard led the farmer to a rock, tapped on it and the rock opened leading to two caves. In the first cave were a large company of sleeping warriors, all but one having a white horse. The wizard placed the horse by the side of this warrior, and then led the farmer into the second cave which was filled with gold and precious stones. The wizard told the farmer to take what he thought was a fair price for the horse and said that one day when the country was in great peril the warriors would awake and ride into battle. The farmer would never find the cave again once he left it. He took a fair price in gold, but when he looked back, as he was riding away, the wizard and the rock had disappeared. An old legend linked former pub names in Alderley Edge stating that should England be invaded, the **Wizard** would bring his army, the **Queen's Hotel** (now offices) would bring the Charter sign, the **Royal Oak** (now **The Oak**) would give the royal command and the **Drum and Monkey** would beat the drum.

WOLVERTON ARMS, Crewe. No sign but worth mentioning as it was built when workers and their families were sent from Wolverton to live in Crewe as a result of one of the mergers of the Grand Junction Railway with other lines in the 1840s. The pub was built to attract their custom.

THE WOODMAN, Macclesfield, has a sign of a man strenuously wielding an axe against a tree. He has already made a large notch in it.

Y

THE YACHT, Mollington. The sign shows a yacht with a red and white full billowing sail. As the pub is near to Shotwick, once a busy port, sailors often frequented it.

The Wizard of Edge, Alderley Edge.

YE OLDE BLACK BEAR, Sandbach. The pub, at the present time, has a sign of a keeper leading a chained bear. Originally called the Black Bear, it was built, according to the inscription, in 1634 on land later owned by Lord Crewe. It has a thatched roof and a half-timbered upper storey. The cellar is reputed to be haunted.

YE OLDE BOOT INN, Chester, situated on the upper part of one of the Chester Rows, is a former merchant's house, dating from 1643, although the front was rebuilt in the nineteenth century. Inside the door can be seen part of the original wattle and daub. The inn was originally confined behind a barber's shop and access was reached by a corridor adjacent to the shop. Above the inn is a parlour going across the Cheshire Row and extending well back. This is one of the largest survivors of such a room in Chester. The inn retains its long low corridor form, with low-beamed ceilings and timbered walls.

YE OLDE CUSTOMS HOUSE INN, Chester. This pub, in a building dating from 1637, and situated on Watergate Street, the principal route from the Wharf, faces the site of the former Custom's House. Chester was a busy port on the west coast until the estuary silted up during the late eighteenth century.

YE OLDE DEVA, Chester. Deva was the Roman name for the fort which preceded the town of Chester. The pub has a fourteenth-century staircase, an inglenook fireplace 350 years old and other features dating to the sixteenth century.

The Yacht, Mollington.

YE OLDE GARDENER ARMS, Broughton. Market gardeners had stalls here 200 years ago. A ghost, reputed to haunt the place, is said to be that of the last man to be beheaded in the county. A monument marking this is across the street.

YE OLDE KINGS ARMS, Congleton. This is probably the oldest surviving building in the town dating back to at least 1585. In the cellars are, what appear to be, bricked-up passageways, which lead to the nearby Town Hall. The sign shows three red lions couchant set on a white shield surmounted by a helmet and helmeted crest; the mantling is merely a feathery design.

YE OLDE KINGS HEAD, Chester. Randle Holmes, Mayor of Chester (1633-34), built this as a private house in 1622. It was occupied by four male generations of the family, all called Randle Holmes, who were heraldry painters and genealogists. Many of their painting of coats of arms are in Cheshire churches. The building was licensed as an inn in 1717. The sign shows the head of Charles I.

YE OLDE NUMBER THREE, Little Bollington. This name refers to the fact that the pub used to be the third coaching stop on the Liverpool-London route. Behind the pub is the Bridgwater Canal. Another explanation is that the pub boasts three ghosts – a poltergeist, a crying child and a female gypsy.

YE OLDE PARK GATE, Over Peover. This is opposite the gates of Peover Hall, which was the headquarters of Generals Patton and Eisenhower for part of the Second World

Ye Olde Black Bear, Sandbach.

War. (*See* **Bells of Peover**.) This was originally a cobbler's shop. Inside is a collection of ladder-backed Macclesfield chairs.

YE OLDE RED COW, Nantwich, has a sign of a placid red cow.

YE OLDE VAULTS, Chester. The pub was licensed in the 1800s. **Ye Olde Union Vaults**, Nantwich, displays a sign showing a vault filled with barrels. A man sits at ease, his pint pot placed on an upturned barrel before him.

YE OLDE WHITE LION, Congleton. The sign depicts a rampant white lion in true heraldic guise. Parts of the building date back to the seventeenth century. It is reputed to have been an attorney's office where John Bradshaw served his articles. He was mayor of the town (1637-38) but later moved to London and as a fervent Roundhead and supporter of Oliver Cromwell, was appointed President of the Court, which tried Charles I. His signature appears on the death warrant of the King. He died in 1658 but after the Restoration his body was dug up and his head was displayed, with those of other regicides, on the roof of Westminster Hall. Sometime in the nineteenth century the front of the building had a white stucco surface but this was removed and the present building has resumed its half-timbered black and white appearance. 'Ma' Skelton, who took over the pub in 1940 after her husband's death, refused to

The Yeoman, Alsager.

have anything to do with modern technology. She fetched the beer from the cellar in two white jugs for mild and in two green jugs for bitter, until her retirement in 1967. The opportunity was quickly taken to refurbish the pub before the next landlord took over. (*See* **White Lion**.)

THE YEOMAN, Alsager. The sign shows a horse leaping up controlled by the rider who is aiming a gun. This was originally the Railway Inn when it was rebuilt in 1848 and was the meeting place of the Ancient Order of Foresters. During the Second World War the Roman Catholics sometimes held Sunday Mass here. When St Gabriel's RC Church was opened, a celebratory lunch was held for the Right Reverend John Murray, Bishop of Shrewsbury. The dishes were appropriately named – *Poisson Gabriel* (after the church), *Glace Velarde* (after the architect F.X. Velarde) and *Pommes Tyson* (after the builders).

Other local titles published by The History Press

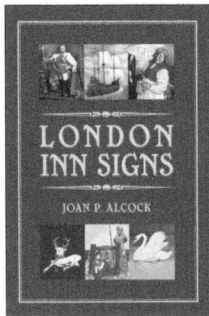

London Inn Signs
JOAN P. ALCOCK

Illustrated with over 100 photographs, this potted history of inn signs from notable historic inns in London offers a fascinating insight into the stories behind the signs. Joan Alcock takes the reader on a tour of inns past and present, discovering the origins of the inn names. The 'pocket book' nature of this book makes it an ideal gift for anyone wanting to follow a historic trail of London's inns, and will especially appeal to local history groups who organise such walks.

978 0 7524 3833 7

Sydenham and Forest Hill History & Guide
JOAN P. ALCOCK

This book describes the development of Sydenham and Forest Hill from open common land in Kent to the sprawling suburb of Greater London that it is today. The well-illustrated guide is a readable introduction to the area's past. It includes a series of walking tours, which reveal the history of the area in its existing streets and buildings.

978 0 7524 3406 3

Congleton
JOAN P. ALCOCK

This collection of more than 180 archive photographs traces some of the many ways in which Congleton has changed and developed over the last hundred years. All aspects of everyday life are recorded here, from shops, businesses, churches and schools to work, leisure, day trips and days off. With images from Congleton Museum, the *Congleton Chronicle* and private collections, this book will reawaken nostalgic memories for many, while offering others a unique glimpse of the past.

978 0 7524 4279 2

Mid-Cheshire Pubs
J. BRIAN CURZON

This collection of over 200 photographs, sketches and paintings provides a pictorial history of the pubs of Mid-Cheshire, taking in Northwich, the Over Ridge, Castle Hill, Sandiway, Middlewich, Winsford and Wharton. This entertaining selection offers an insight into the buildings, names, and drinkers of the Mid-Cheshire pubs and will appeal to everyone who enjoy a good tale and a drink.

978 0 7524 3852 8

If you are interested in purchasing other books published by The History Press, or in case you have difficulty finding any History Press books in your local bookshop, you can also place orders directly through our website:

www.thehistorypress.co.uk